LOVING CANDACE

MARVIN COHEN

EDITED BY COLIN MYERS

Parts of this book previously appeared in the following publications:

— *Run Out Of Prose* (Sagging Meniscus, 2018)
— *Sadness Corrected* (Sagging Meniscus, 2019)
— *Conversations and Versifications* (Tough Poets, 2021)
— *thecollidescope.com* (June 1, 2021)
— *Trying to Fool Death* (Tough Poets, 2023)
— *How, Upon Reflection, to be Amorous* (Sagging Meniscus, 2023)
— *Exacting Clam #11: Winter 2023*

Our thanks to Rebecca Watt for contributing a biographical sketch of Candace Watt, and for permission to reproduce family photographs.

© 2024 by Marvin Cohen

All Rights Reserved.

Set in Janson with LaTeX.

ISBN: 978-1-963846-14-0 (paperback)
Library of Congress Control Number: 2024943255

Sagging Meniscus Press
Montclair, New Jersey
saggingmeniscus.com

For Candace Watt

March 8, 1937 – September 22, 2023

Contents

A Glimpse of Candace Watt, by Rebecca Watt	*vi*
How Marvin Met Candace	*viii*
Loving Candace	*1*
Of Friends and Other Memories	*129*
Afterword	*203*

A GLIMPSE OF CANDACE WATT

Candace Quinby Watt (CQW) was born in Hartford, Connecticut on March 8, 1937 and grew up mainly in New Haven. Her father Thomas was born in Edinburgh, Scotland, moved to the USA at 25 years old and worked as an accountant. Her mother Cyrena (born in New Haven Connecticut and with a maternal heritage in New Haven going back to the 1600s) studied art history at Yale and later set up an 'Epicurean' catering business.

CQW graduated from Swarthmore College in 1959 with a degree in English, a lasting love of literature (from Chaucer to Agatha Christie) and a particular penchant for satire. After a year at Yale Public Library she went to New York and worked at the publishers W.W. Norton, where she became editor of the paperback department, until her retirement about 2008.

CQW and Marvin met in the early 1970s, their paths crossing in NYC's literary world. Over time it just seemed the natural thing to do to be married, as they became on May 22, 1986.

They shared many things together: a love of music (from classical to Gilbert and Sullivan), films, art, a love of words, a strong support for the Democratic Party and food (CQW, a love of cooking; Marvin, a formidable appetite, though he, himself, couldn't boil water).

Other things they tolerated in one another: her strong Christian faith and his militant atheism; his devotion to baseball, cricket and other sports and her virtual indifference.

As a person she had a sharp intellect, wit and humour, a warmth that made her a good listener, though with a sometimes brutal honesty and perhaps a tendency to be overly self-critical. In her support, Marvin Cohen gave her the gift of really loving her and respecting her as she was, which she reciprocated with a total commitment to their relationship.

A GLIMPSE OF CANDACE WATT

Candace suffered ill health for many years, inexorably losing her ability to see and to breathe. She finally succumbed and let go of life on September 22, 2023, in Manhattan, NYC. Her loss has left an immeasurable hole in the hearts of those who loved her, primarily her beloved husband Marvin, as well as myself.

—*Rebecca Watt (Candace's younger sister)*

Candace and Rebecca Watt

HOW MARVIN MET CANDACE

GS: I'm curious, how did you meet Candace?

MC: There was a party I crashed and I met her that way. Parties are often where things happened.

GS: How long ago was that? Do you remember?

MC: Well, maybe some time in the late '70s and now it's 2021, so that's a long time ago.

GS: Wow. I read somewhere that she was "a retired paperback editor."

MC: Yeah, of W.W. Norton publishers. [. . .]

GS: Did she ever edit your work?

MC: No.

GS: Did you ever ask her for advice or anything like that?

MC: No, because I'm about six years older and I had already, by the time I met her, experience in getting published and so I already found my own voice. Already editing my stuff.

[From 'Fame and Fortune,' MC in conversation with George Salis, thecollidescope.com]

LOVING CANDACE

LOVING CANDACE

MARRIAGE CYCLE (IN 4 PARTS)

1. TO MY WIFE, IN ACRID SWEETNESS

Occasional flareups will be dampened and subdued
between me and my lady love.
Nature gave to us on earth
what the birds easily have above.
My heart pours out such assistance
as her physical troubles demand
that my whole being is the physician
to keep my bird flying on the land.
Between us, our pulses flicker and stand.

2. MY WIFE, IN ALL HER YEARS

The tears I occasionally let descend
all in my wife's behalf
are for her troubles in eyes and lungs.
She's glad to have me there.
I pour out mercy from my heart
that has no medical talent.
Compassion lightens out of my eyes;
and so, to paraphrase along with Yeats,
and modern-eyes his tune,
I louder sing, the more tatters in her mortal dress.

3. I HELP MYSELF TO WHAT THE WORLD CAN GIVE

If my wife, who's occasionally tart,
distills her sweetness to the world,
only a few friends and relatives respond.
And so do I, as long as my might
derives energy from the world's hidden love
that bursts out, blazes above.

4. WE BICKER. OKAY, BUT SO WHAT?

Is love intangible?
Of course. But symbolized by real things.
So that can barely suggest
that I love, but not in jest,
my actual true-life love
called by marriage my wife,
as sociology or society unites
the two of us into proverbially one
despite occasional disputes.
Though we argue like brutes,
our beings couple and click wings.
Love is composed of such real things.
I flutter my heart-wrapped song
to my wife who quite kisses me along
and lectures me on what's wrong.

MY LIFE, MY WIFE

I love Candace Watt, who's my wife.
For better or worse, I've shared my life
for the last fifty years
(producing many laughs and tears)
with this same woman into mutual old age,
always in the same book, on the occasional different page.
We've been through all kinds of stresses
but always with commitments to the same addresses,
where our love enlarges as it progresses,
bearing up with some understandable stresses
which each of us in turn addresses.
In short, she means all of love to me,
worth it all through the payment of any fee.

A CONSTANT TRIBUTE

Who do I care about a lot?
She's my wife, Candace Watt.
Of her many attributes,
she's serious, but full of cutes,
though old age now wilts her down,
but me too, we share the same crown,
and will be together always
while life in our veins still plays.
I commend us to further sweet days
while longevity blesses us and stays.

**DEATH AND LOVE
ARE A WEIRD COMBINATION
TO SUSTAIN IN ALTERNATION**

Candace Watt is my lovely wife.
Occasionally we have spasms of strife.
She's learning to walk again.
The constant home-health aids are expensive.
I love her more and more
as the past recedes and the future looms,
and all the dust is swept with brooms.
Let's live and die together;
she's my future and my past.
How long will we last?

LET'S OPPOSE DEATH
WITH OUR ALTERNATE RHYTHM OF BREATH

Death is a frightening prospect
so far as anyone can detect.
Life is more precious loving Candace Watt,
but now the two of us are on the spot.
Let's struggle to live longer,
because my love is already much stronger.

PRAISING CANDACE WATT
TO SUCH SUFFICIENCY, IT'S A LOT

Who or what
charms like Candace Watt?
She's the opposite to a blood clot
that dooms the vessels to be shot.
If you love her, it's quite a lot
for her to bear, no matter what.
I signed our marriage pact to every dot,
and look at my sweet darling whom I got!

RETURNING A COMPLIMENT
EASY AS A CANDY CONDIMENT
SWALLOWED LIKE IT'S SURELY MEANT
IN A DELICIOUS INTENT
ACCORDING TO OUR TASTE'S BENT

Loving Candace Watt
is like connecting every dot
without making a blot.
I ask her what
her charm is due to,
but she only proclaims, "You too!"

**LOVING CANDACE WATT
AFTER WE'VE TIED THE KNOT
AND CONSTRUED OUR LIFE PATH PLOT**

Love for Candace Watt
is an act I'll never blot.
She supplies the "who" and "what,"
but only I supply the "why."
How my love to her does fly!
It holds up the whole sky
just to come winging by
to drop me off to see her.
What does it take to be her?
She controls her own essence.
Cork off, watch the effervescence!

**TO CANDACE WATT
WHO'S CONNECTED MY DOT
ALL OVER THE LOT**

By love we're attached,
so it's a mutual catch
to open the latch
for a suitable love match
punctuated by a kiss and hug
to catch the pesky love bug.
Candace Watt and I
are eye to eye together
tightly woven in a tether.
Come out and feel the weather.
We're an acceptable duo,
and our bloods' traffic will flow
any which way to stay
the way we are; at long last
we've built our love to last
through the lulls and through the blast.
For this ride we clutch fast.

LOVE'S FEELING
IN CANDID REVEALING

To love is to feel close,
and it must be kept that way,
not to withdraw.
You really need that person,
and desperately hope likewise
that she requites you
with similar desperation
or approximately so.
You really can't do without her,
and count that she feels the same way.
Being with her is not monotonous,
but is full of meaning
that never quite dulls;
an addiction without poisoning,
that approximates wonderful fiction
of superb interestingness
that never really grows any less.
Having her within your sight
increases your powerful might
to fulfill your reassurance
that there she is for you:
a stable state of affairs.
It's real, she's there,
as needed as constant breath
to keep guard against death.
Within you, she's quite concealed
as your private "must."
You're helpless without that trust.
Your love is a happy blessing
that shouts pride in confessing.

A LIVE LOVE AND ONE DEAD.
THEY BOTH GO TO MY HEAD

to Candace Watt:

I approximate understanding you
and try empathy too.
I sympathize and identify
with what you go through.
But still you're a foreign object,
yet I love you, you're mine.
How did we two combine?

to Jimmy Stagno:

Jimmy Stagno was my friend
for seventy years, a long end
from early adolescence.
We laughed with words of eloquence
and loved to play baseball,
later pool, and loved each other,
riding in your car and walking,
and always talking, but now
you're the dead one. Where am I with you?
You were so real. Is it true?

**TYPES OF NATURE'S LOVE
FROM DEEP BELOW OR FROM ABOVE,
THE WAY THE FINGERS FIT IN A GLOVE
AND THE LADY BIRD LOVES HER DOVE**

Loving Candace is easy.
The tree loves the wind if it's breezy.
Trees love their roots in the ground,
barking that "roots are profound."
The birds love the air to fly in,
with gifted wings to do the job,
and have enough space to avoid the mob.
The squirrel loves the tree to climb up
from branch to slimmer twigs,
the better to search for figs.
Bald men naturally take to wigs.
The flowers love insects with pollen,
whether the leaves bloom or have fallen.
The fish love the sea to swim in.
Obesity loves diet to slim in.
Candace is easy to love.
Nature reigns on us from above
and from the ground level too.
Loving Candace is automatic.
She won't let me be autocratic.

**LOVE'S DEFINITION
THAT STICKS TO ITS POSITION
AND RESISTS ALL OPPOSITION**

Of all things, what's love?
The state of being above,
because of the other.
Otherwise, why bother?
It's as easy to love Candace
as to stifle a wound with a bandage,
or at least feast when you're famished,
so your relationship won't be damaged.
And somehow you'll both manage,
even resorting to carnage,
but smoothing it over with varnish.

MY TWO CANDACE WATTS. WHICH IS WHICH, AND WHO'S WHAT'S?

First there was the real you,
and then the memory came to life.
Which was which and who was who?
Time danced in between us:
The real you was the one I loved.
But memory stood in for you
like an actress playing a role.
She did a reasonable facsimile
and owned my double stage:
my passion roused to a rage.
Now I have you both, back and forth.
You take turns; my love is reinforced.
I take a double scoop, I take a double course.
I can't do without either:
the healthy germ and the healthy fever:
the original, and the continual retriever.
So memory serves a good purpose:
I get the depth, and I get the surface.
The memory provides the essence,
and then there's the real presence.

MY LOVE OF CANDACE WATT
BEGS THE QUESTION OF WHAT'S WHAT

When I look at my wife, Candace Watt,
I seem to adore her a lot.
But that's between me and her:
the mystery of what makes the cat purr.
Having been with her a long time
completes the puzzle of the necessary rhyme.
Having enjoyed her acquaintance much
gives us both a familiar touch.
Whenever we come face to face,
the clock roars and we rush to grace.
Like truck drivers on the long haul,
we've circumnavigated the familiar ball
of minutes, days, and years
to find out how life appears
and also what's its essence.
We've become dependent on each other's presence.
It's still full of wholesomeness
that rescues us from dolefulness.
When each one enters the room,
we're glad we had once been wife and groom,
and allow each other to generously assume
what nature, art, and politics are
under our common living star.

**FAREWELL TO A GREAT COUPLE
WHOSE MARRIAGE PROVED SO SUPPLE,
IT PERSISTED WITHOUT DISRUPTAL,
BUT WITH AN OCCASIONAL GRUMBLE
WITHIN THE MARITAL FOREST OR JUNGLE**

My love of Candace Watt
is dearly deep in upshot.
She has a slim, cute figure,
but mine is appropriately bigger.
We met and launched a later romance,
as each took a breathless, hesitant stance.
Was it inevitable that we married, perchance?
Possibly. So we're in for the long haul,
like truck drivers whose far away distances never appall.
From past to future we've stretched afar,
so brevity was not a factor in our eternal star.
Were Candace and I made for each other?
Life together was great. Could we have another?
No. Our mutual greed would smother.
So it's nearly time that we have to die.
Whose tears come first, taking turns to cry?
The one who mourns will say "Good night,"
as the other takes their leave in perilous flight.
Let's bid farewell to both,
to honor their long-ago troth
wherein they took persuasive oath
too late for vigorous youth,
but enough to convey their double-edged truth.

WOOING CANDACE WATT,
BUT TOO POOR TO OWN A YACHT

Such a lovely woman is Candace Watt
that I'd like to take her on a yacht,
but alas I've insufficient money
to so indulge my sweet dear honey.
So cancel that unused trip
on the yacht, and skip
all the preliminaries of going to sea
for the ostentatious purpose of boasting a yacht
just to impress Candace Watt.
Can't I impress her by myself alone
as a simple loving human being
feeling fit and exerting charm?
That's what I humbly offer. Would it do her harm?
Now she knows that money isn't everything,
we'll seek cheaper methods for joy to bring.
The glittering fascinations of enormous wealth
dissolve to nothing compared to two people's health.

**TO CANDACE AN EPISTLE
WHICH IF SHE GRANTS, I'LL WHISTLE
NOT TO TURN ON MYSELF A PISTOL**

When Candace takes me for granted,
I'll mention a sculptor who sculpted in granite,
but also sculpted in marble.
As a sculptor, he was a marvel.
So don't you ever take me for granted.
In your mind I've often planted
the idea of what a great guy I am.
Believe me literally, or else I'll scram
and punish you by not giving a damn.
So if you want to retain my love,
join me at the heights here above,
and condescend to so kiss me true and true
to convey not only my love for you,
but also your love sublime
that sweetly I may dearly call mine.
Such motivation is this bottom line.

LET ME BE CANDID ABOUT HOW I MET CANDACE. WHAT LUCK! IT WAS THE GRANDEST

Having known Candace Watt,
I really hit the jackpot!
I met her right on the spot,
by accident at a party
which was somewhat arty.
She gave me a platter of food
that requited my hungry mood.
I ate up her shining presence,
and this was fortune's greatest present.
I still enjoy her in the present.
She really had me smashed.
The party? I had crashed,
not knowing the host or hostess.
But Candace proved to be the mostest.
Compared to her, others are the grossest.
Our meals are furnished at the grocer's.
Between us, I eat the mostest.
Love itself has become our new hostess.
We're worn out, and need the most rest.
But time itself will do the arrest,
due to death's earnest quest.

LEAVE LOVE ALONE.
IT'S DOUBLY KEPT, NOT ON LOAN

Loving Candace is reinforced by getting loved back,
so I know that I'm on the right track.
Equality is good in democracy
of having equal rights.
So may Candace and I never have fights,
except some that are easily made up,
so she and I will fill each other's cup
with wine full flowing to the end.
Love gets you drunk when it never needs to mend.
Such a love I recommend.
What's the middle, when love is from both sides to send?
Why fiddle with what's all right?
There's nowhere to go but to have a fight.
Thus we pretend, and toy around,
while love keeps firm on its solid ground.
Thus we keep aloft, pound for pound.

HERE'S ALL THE WHAT'S WHAT
OF ME AND CANDACE WATT,
NEGATING PEOPLE'S NEED TO ASK WHAT

Loving Candace Watt
is not a load of rot.
We never had a tot,
being married late,
and slow off the gate.
An ancestry like a Scot
gave her strawberry blond hair.
But that's neither here nor there.
Her soul is big as the globe.
No wonder we had to elobe,
and then were soon to grobe.
Thus all romances evolve,
like plumbers know their valve
of faucets hot or cold.
Knowledge makes us bold
with complete authority,
akin to enlightened morality.
We can dispense with formality
and get on with nitty gritty,
taking excursions into being witty
while keeping up with feeding the kitty.
How privileged, living in the City!
Sophistication is our product
as a real grown-up adult,
thus determining our conduct.
Enjoying life together
occurs independent of weather.
We're not freaky. (We don't wear leather.)
We're frequently apart,

but never threaten to part,
and unlikely ever to start.
Love has deepened
through the years,
and its volume is never in arrears.

**MY DEBT TO CANDACE WATT
AS WELL AS JOHN DONNE.
THUS MY ACKNOWLEDGEMENTS ARE DONE,
GIVING ME RHETORICAL FUN**

I owe her a life debt.
Will I pay it? You bet.
She so contributed to my welfare
that to pay her back is only fair.
People stare at me in her glare.
She made me feel secure
and took away anxiety.
Yet she was modest and demure,
and well adept at society
with its inestimable variety.
Without my wife, what would I have done?
Go on trying to imitate John Donne.
He was such a metaphysical poet
that he wanted the whole world to know it.
As far as putting words together, he could show it.
When he ran out of inspiration, he might blow it.
So now that my poem is hereby done,
I've finished my clumsy praise of John Donne.

AN APPEAL TO DEATH
TO SPARE US BOTH IN THE SAME BREATH

I don't dare do my loving wife harm,
she in her mid eighties and I ninety-one.
May death give our love one more year
of mercy's grace despite our double fear.
I offer this economy bargain,
so please delay unruly barging.
Don't heap fatality on us both
to break our solemn double oath
and stunt our lengthy aging growth.

CANDACE

After many married years, your wife died.
At first you got relief when you cried.
But those wet tears were only superficial.
To make it gravely official, I felt grief,
which was deeper and more serious than mere relief.
To say that I merely missed her was not enough.
Memory comes in many shapes and forms.
Illusions and delusions fell away from the norms.
Insanity ruled my psychology,
deeper than the earth's geography.
I couldn't get her out of my mind.
But her constant images made me blind
to any proportion or perspective.
She was mine, retrospective.
Love was always our elective.
She's not there, but love is immense
and never-endingly intense.
Oh dear Candace, I loved you so.
I want you to cling and never let go.
Our love was so real,
it's still the way I always feel.
Actually, it grows bolder
the more I behold her.

**MY SWEET WIFE IS THE ONLY ONE
TO RECEIVE MY BEST PUN**

I love my wife: Candace Watt.
If her speech is difficult to hear, I ask "What?"
That's the best practical pun I could make
that she's perfectly able to take.
I do it for my own sake,
because of the sweet smile on her cute face.
She's a symbol of loveliness and grace.
So if I mishear, I ask her "What?"
to award my best pun to Candace Watt.

WATCHING MY WIFE

(1)

I love my wife, but she's dying,
so naturally I'm crying.
I remember how good things were in the past.
The contrast is too strong to grasp.
I stand by helpless while she's fading.
Nothing I can do to be aiding.
She has a helpless woe on her face.
The oxygen tank is helping her breathe.
Her stomach is too gnarled up to feed.
Love pours out from my soul.
Is it our fault that we get old?

(2)

Love is flowing through my veins,
but horribly in vain.
The old days are giving me pain.
Her eyes are closing periodically.
The darkness is closing in.
I'm with her, together.
She doesn't want to be touched.
I'm isolated.
She's desperate. I'm alone.
We can't use the telephone
or any other instrument.
I wipe my many tears
and remember those years.

MY WIFE IS IN EMERGENCY.
HOW CAN I RESPOND TO THIS URGENCY?

My wife is going crazy.
Normally she's as sweet as a daisy.
But she has outrageous dreams
and is coming apart at the seams.
Nothing is quite as it seems.
She hears voices from outside the window,
and they all sound threatening.
She can't normally breathe without injecting oxygen.
I hope she's not on her last limb.
She accuses the home health aides
of plotting to murder her.
Her mind is in unruly shape.
How can it get back in order
if she's already crossed the border?

ME AND CANDACE
ARE BEING CANDID,
BUT NOT NECESSARILY FRANTIC

Candace Watt loves me,
and I love her.
Both of us are like cats,
which we know may well infer
that cats protect their fur
and people their skin,
so we know what breed we're in.
Each of us fears Death
with deep guardians over our breath
that operates through old age
before dropping in on Death's containing cage,
not without a burst of rage,
hugging each other on the same page,
mutually forever to engage.
Death would not spare us either,
but allowed each an occasional breather
till the climactic event
that neither Candace nor I are ever able to prevent
to any appreciable extent.

**CANDACE WATT
WAS THE BEST THING I GOT.
DO I MISS HER? MUCH MORE THAN A LOT.
BUT IT'S TOO LATE NOW TO MAKE A PLOT**

Candace Watt is dead and gone,
dear enough to weep upon,
memory by memory to weep some more
how we would deeply love and adore.
We were married for fifty years.
Now I'm in my nineties and alone,
save for friends galore
to joke with and fool around,
and occasionally go to town.
What can compensate for Candace Watt?
Nothing. I go on weeping,
but her soul is with me, only sleeping.
We hold imaginary hands
and re-travel former lands,
and gossip about friends in common
whom only each other's company can summon.
One half of it is me.
She's the other, wretchedly free.

LOSING CANDACE
OFFSETS MY MENTAL BALANCE
DESPITE MY TENUOUS TALENTS

I loved Candace with all my heart,
but her death makes us part.
Death is decisive and proactive,
making life its captive.
I can still envisage us kissing,
but something is missing.
Death is the cause of this outrage
that wipes our lifelong romance off the stage.
I decline from belief to grief,
with tears my outlet.
Am I miserable? You bet.
It's a permanent regret.
Candace is no longer there.
She's wiped away, in clean air.
I remain here, holding the bag,
lamenting my remaining lag.
Love life's dogged tail will no longer wag,
and I'll not rejoin Candace despite my sag.

HOW LOVE TOOK A BACK SEAT, MAKING MY LIFE PREMATURELY INCOMPLETE

Candace and I loved each other more and more
after a fifty-year marriage,
but her viral pneumonia crippled her lungs
with bronchiectasis (chronic enlargement of bronchial tubes).
So our love at its zenith had to take a back seat
to swallowing her indigestible saliva,
and her lovely face was cleaned up as a hospital ornament corpse.
Heartbroken, I learned my lesson
that sentimental love can't sing its lyrical song
when the progress of viral pneumonia crippled her lungs,
and our darling heartbroken love had to give way
to the stronger argument of physical decay.
So her death became a thief
of our love, forcing me into grief
that keeps up its barren song.
Her broken body and I just couldn't get along.
There's no heaven, so I resume my life
after Candace's physical ordeal of love-broken strife.

GRIEF

Oh Candace, where are you?
You're invisible to the naked eye,
and with snotty tears I have to cry,
when on the phone I said "I love you,"
and you responded: "I love you too."
Could two old lovebirds survive?
You didn't, because of severe disease
that led to your unavoidable decease.
I love you forever with all my heart,
death having taken too greedy a part.
I love you forever, dear Candace.
I'll miss you forevermore,
with nothing available for us to restore.
I take the burden alone,
and I adore you, every single bone,
including your sweet skull
that managed not to find me dull.

**CANDACE IS BEYOND
MY ABILITY TO BE FOND.
NO WONDER SHE CAN'T RESPOND**

I love Candace Watt,
but she's already dead,
so hope is fled
that she'll love me back.
Dead people are unable to love,
being below instead of above.
They're so fatally passive
as to be merely a stiff,
so they can't even act "as if."
Thus I remain the one loving.
Tears gather in my eyes
to know that my beloved is beyond surprise.
So I can't move her no matter how I devise.
So all I can do is stay still
to imitate her, but it makes me ill
and wish that she still has a will
to respond to me,
for which I dare not plea.
But no signal can she give to me,
so my tears may now be wrenched free
and spill out in grief
like a lonely Autumn leaf.

LOVE MISSING
INSTEAD OF KISSING

I miss Candace so much
because we're beyond mutual touch.
Any part of her skin
would enable me to win.
But nothing of her is presentable.
That's the thing that's contemptible.
She's only a mere ghost
of whose company I can't boast.
She doesn't materialize
in any literal size,
like in a burst of surprise.
Then she'd be a sight for sore eyes,
which would open so wide
that I'd hug her to my side
and join her on what to decide,
and our absences we'd describe
of how we missed each other,
but now we have one another.
The feeling would be mutual bliss.
If only I could experience this!
But not, I'm reduced to tears
and wonder how many years.

HISTORY WITH CANDACE:
HERE'S A CONDENSED CANVAS

Candace was my one and only wife,
but now she just lost her own life
due to chronic lung disease
that viralled its way to her decease.
I miss her so much,
that it's not only like losing touch.
My heart is the thing that's hurt,
due to her emotional worth.
It was not merely a married romance,
but we were in a full lifetime trance,
hugging closely at the dance.
Yet I had enough time to do my writing,
so enough privacy was her gift to me
to set me literarily free.
So if I manage to achieve fame,
I'll give her credit as assistance to my aim,
since she paid for rent and expenses,
and I was her devoted parasite,
living at close quarters on the same site,
and she treated me not only extraordinarily, but right.
But hardly once did we ever have a serious fight.
My life without her might have been an awful plight,
since I was chronically poor,
and had enough complexities to endure,
in which I bumbled and was not sure.
And also I was seriously semi-deaf,
which didn't interfere with my true emotional depth.

I LEAVE HER AT THE HOSPITAL
TOO DEAD TO BE COMFORTABLE

With her Roman profile and mouth agape,
she lay on the hospital bed
for "viewing,"
instead of renewing.
She was a corpse on exhibition
in the posthumous position
of blank disposition.
I blindly churn out my tears
as her spirit gently disappears
into the rear view of departing years.

WHY HER DEATH VIRTUALLY KILLS ME

(1)

Within our fifty-year marriage, we grew to more special
feelings for one another, till at the end our love increased
on both sides, till it grew in intensity to two-way specialties,
only for death to break up the combined organism into her
death part and my grieving part.

(2)

One is alive, the other is dead.
How can that organism get ahead?
It lacks self-harmony.
So what's the harm in me,
that neither shares the same state
to realize the perfect fate
as an exquisitely ideal mate?

THE VOW

Just before death, Candace vowed eternal love,
putting us both there—above.
Thus her death presided over her vow,
with the perfect gem it would allow.
I wept my way into grief,
which never gave me relief.
Sprawled across her hospital bed,
I snatched a kiss before she fled,
and my heart immediately bled.
For the second time, we were wed.
Our souls in twin-ship swiftly arose
into the heavens in repose.
There we were, man and wife,
far above mutual strife.
Dear Candace, armed with your vow,
our new status makes me go "Wow!"
In virtual terms, it's forever,
making our parting never.
To seal that vow was eternally clever.
Only divinity would have inspired it ever.

SAD STATEMENT

I miss Candace, but nothing I can do about it. Death is a tough adversary never to be overcome, so I have to suffer till I finally get used to her permanent absence. How many times has this fatal predicament been enacted by people, the world over in all languages? I myself, being ninety-two, am helplessly vulnerable. Life is so precious. Loving your departed one is so tragic. I can never stop loving her, and will carry her death into my own.

HER FINAL EMACIATED DAYS

The more her wrecked body was collapsing, the more frequently we avowed that our love for each other, over many years of marriage, had increased in leaps and bounds, seemingly miraculously.

So I visited her at the hospital desperately for our last gleams of eternal love, and managed sprawlingly to scrawl kisses over her reclining lips, while she uttered weak words I couldn't hear.

Later that day, her ruined lungs gave way by choking on her food.

Alerted, I returned to the hospital to see her cleaned-up profile, mouth agape, on the viewing bed.

The horror gave way to grief, which somehow never stops. Now my grief is her substitute companion.

DEATH DIALOGUE

Can anything humorous be made out of death?
Yes, if you're in the right mood.
Do you want to try it now?
No. Candace died last week.
So you're too miserable to joke about death?
No. This is the very wrong time.
But will you snap out of it?
(Glumly:) Eventually, I suppose.
Boy, do you sound gloomy!
Under the circumstances, why not?
Is that as far as you can go?
But not so far as she went.

THE LOSS OF CANDACE
GAVE ME SHOCK AND PANIC

Candace's terrible lung disease
led to her horrible decease
to choke on her saliva,
and she's no longer aliv-a.
Down went our love in doom,
petrifying me in gloom.
Death wielded its magic,
and we ended up tragic.
Our love was at its peak,
but now it's only me to seek,
suffocating with grief
that affords me no relief.
I loved her with all my heart.
Thanks to death's demonic art,
we're driven dramatically apart,
and our memories rush endlessly to start,
minus her defunct brain,
leaving me all the pain
that my insides must drain.
This is too metaphysical to explain,
since it leaves nothing quite plain.
Further meditation leaves no gain.
All we're left with is love,
whose location is strictly above.

**AN EPITAPH
IN ITS FINAL DRAFT**

Poor Candace is gone
with nothing to be beyond.
She leaves as my life's love,
directionally "above."
I carry her as part of me,
complete with unified memory
so far as I could see.
The rest is laden with mystery,
and depends on our former history.
But here it is, point blank:
I have mostly her choking to thank
to make "widower" be my rank.
All of Candace I loved so much,
that I yearn just for her casual touch,
and treat it as sacred as such.
Then I choke and weep in the clutch.

WHAT FLOWERS HOPED FOR
WHEN PEOPLE WOULD PASS BEFORE

When Candace and I were in the Brooklyn Botanic Gardens,
passing by the flowers, we didn't have to say pardons,
although the flowers would wave
because they seemed to crave
attention to their beauty
as if it were the people's duty.
Whether tulips, lilacs, or daffodils,
the flowers would get thrills
that their beauty was so admired
that people would never get tired
of giving aesthetic praise
to the flowers that the Brooklyn Botanic Gardens would raise.

BELATED APOLOGY ABOUT THEOLOGY

I always loved Candace,
but took her for granted
when doubtful argument was planted
by my misbehavior
in criticizing her Savior.
She believed in Christianity,
for which I had nothing but profanity.
Thus, insulting her belief
made me an arrogant thief
of her peace and harmony.
Looking back, I regret the harm in me
that spoiled her mental security
with my vile and nasty impurity.
I wish I could somehow atone
for the brutality of my atheistic tone,
which cost poor Candace an innocent groan.
She couldn't help it. It was the way she was grown.

EPITAPH FOR CANDACE

Loving Candace with all my heart,
we had to part
due to Death's destructive art.
She had a terrible lung disease
that led to her decease.
She choked on her saliva
and was no longer aliv-a.
I'm her miserable survivor.
All the good times we had
were made even more glad
when we were the joint enjoyers,
temporarily avoiding Death's destroyers
when they were not yet our annoyers.
Candace and I were a pair,
but this time she's not there
to capture our good air.

A MARRIAGE OVER FIFTY YEARS CONTRIBUTES TO MY LONELY TEARS

I love Candace so much
that I yearn for her touch,
especially since she died recently,
from which I haven't recovered decently.
I'm overwhelmed by our memories,
of which I'm the only custodian.
I haven't recovered from our history
which, though factual, is still a mystery
detached from recollection.
It all whoozed by so fast,
is it still a real part of my past?
It seems like ancient magic
that my tears recall as tragic.
I'm no longer part of a married couple,
but is my memory sufficiently supple
to separate events into their components?
Her death is the worst of opponents.
I carry our love still
in the process of my single will.
Candace is all over my mind,
but what I'm seeing is blackly blind.
Tears wet my juicy eyes,
telling me her death is no surprise
as she deeply fades into the sunrise.

AFTER CANDACE DIED, THE WORLD WAS ILL SUPPLIED

Lacking the love of Candace,
I've lost my emotional balance.
Without her, I wasn't completed,
so that all my faults would be deleted,
and my virtues so happily seated.
Love is a powerful emotion
where your energies are gathered into motion,
harnessed by the same loving woman
who renders you into a whole full man
to give your all as much as you can
out to the utmost of your span.
Thus you can biologically fulfill her
and saddle her with a baby who will thrill her,
provided it actually will occur
and not fizz out into a phantom blur.
When your adored one has a baby,
it removes the doubt from "maybe,"
and creates such a positive entity
to signify her identity
with the invitation: "any time you want, you can enter me
right into the center of me."
It adds a verbal stress
into the meaning of the word "yes,"
ornamented by the plus of "bless"
to give you the loveliest excess.

CANDACE AND I

I love Candace Watt, but she recently died in constant lung pain.
Our fifty-year marriage built up to maximum love at the end.
To love a dead person has no end till I die myself.
To put us both in the same negative bracket
is to make life very imperfect as a racket.
My last thoughts may or may not be of her.
Who knows what spontaneity may occur?
To associate love with her name
is to vindicate my life as a personal fame
just privately, for us alone.
What will go through my skull bone?

THE FINAL WORDS

Goodbye, Candace, we met an end,
but we weren't aware of it
till I kissed you the night before
in the rigid hospital,
and you said: "I love you too."
That was the beginning of grief
that had its own private relief.
I went into the world first time without you,
but it happily remained never without you.
You were there in person. How could I doubt you?

THE LAST OF MANY WORDS
WERE LIKE A HUMAN FLIGHT OF BIRDS

When Candace and I said goodbye
at the hospital, "I love you too"
were her final words
which at the time we never knew.
In time they became perfectly true,
and fit the bill as literature went,
being our final vocal event.
How maudlin to call it heaven-sent!
I must reserve a much more severe rigor
to sum up our life together with vigor.
We both went bravely off the stage
consecrating our sentiments to old age.
Old age was our perfect meeting place
where in dice or cards I threw down an ace.
But hers were the last words that rang
when the gentle angels flocked together and sang.

THE TREAT WAS ALL MINE, YET IT APPLIED TO BOTH. WE HAD PLIGHTED OUR TROTH

I said goodbye to Candace Watt
for the last time, but it was the last shot
of conversation between us.
Was it mere banality when she said: "I love you too"?
No, it had made my day
when Candace uttered such a say.
It was such a fitting climax
that it was hardly having to pay income tax.
My life was justly fulfilled
in matching what we both willed.
The goose pimples made my flesh chilled.
I danced with such delight, that the ozone was killed,
and the residue was easily spilled.
Never were such perfect words arranged
when the temperature of our time had to be changed.

A CHRONICLE

Meeting Candace was a lucky break.
She would give and I would take.
She was generous with free food,
for whose opulence I was always in the mood
as long as someone else paid,
and had the added advantage to be a pretty maid.
Thus I rapidly fell in love
and reached the heights as a romantic dove.
Too rich had met with too poor,
which was a perfect union for love to endure,
and to be for chronic poverty a cure.
Oh what an opportunity!
I would grab it with impunity,
with the desperation of mutiny.
Then I would grow fat so fast
that my thin self had already passed,
and wouldn't mind another repast.
In what category would he be classed?

**WHO BUT CANDACE
WOULD HAVE A BETTER BALANCE
WHEN YOU CONSIDER ALL HER TALENTS?**

Overseeing my fifty years of married life,
I'd say that they converged with the right wife.
I'm proud to be thus paired.
How with anyone else would I have fared?
Anyone else would have been the wrong story
and be shoved into another category.
But Candace was a real person
as opposed to anyone else's phony version,
on which I would have cast aspersion.
With whom of all mortals other than Candace Watt
would have been more appropriate to cast my lot?
Not an awful lot.
So Candice was so unique
that to marry anyone else would have left me morbid and bleak,
with divorce in the works for next week.
She's left me solid and strong,
and attends to my soul to struggle along,
weaving in my head the right poetic song,
editorializing direct in front,
and if I'm wrong, she's blunt,
and so gets away with that stunt.

DIVIDED

A chronic lung disease
caused Candace to decease.
As her husband, I'm full of grief
that doesn't spare me any relief.
Her images rack my brain
with continual pain.
The separation is intolerable
and worse than horrible,
from my point of view
as how our relationship grew.
What consolation can there be?
Nothing for her, nothing for me.

TRAGEDY'S TERRIFIED STRIFE

My love for Candace Watt is very strong,
but weak enough not to protect her from Death.
So Candace managed to survive my extreme love,
but against Death she was a pushover,
and merely tumbled over
when Death dared to breathe upon her
from her own chronic lung disease,
leading to her horrible decease
and my extreme fit of unease
consisting of depression, grief, and mourning.
If that's not enough, then "good morning"
to anyone reading this.
Death is a tragedy afflicting Candace and me, though I stay alive,
too weak in misery over my lovely wife
caught up in malicious non-existence's strife.
My question is: "Why can't we still share life?"
Why does there have to be a sudden surprise
as if violent dawn terrified its own sunrise?

THE PARTIAL RECOVERY
IS MY NEW DISCOVERY

Since Candace is dead and I'm alive,
I'll miss her, but I'll survive.
I can't keep pining away
with frustration's anguish.
My love for Candace will never languish,
but I've got to be manly and realistic,
so that a modicum of discipline will stick.
Candace Watt is irretrievably dead,
so bring it realistically to your head.
Accept the "impossible-to-be-otherwise,"
and start off again to resume your enterprise.
Gather your old resources
into vital new courses
from impeccable sources.
Start life off on a new phase,
and you'll deserve a warm applause of praise
to make the magnificently most of your days,
letting yourself in for sweet sunrays.

HOW CANDACE REMAINS

After fifty years married to Candace,
her death pulverized me with grief
from which I still lack relief.
Does love inflate its worth?
Emotionally, there's no measure
of my loss of her treasure.
It far exceeds pleasure.
Therefore, Candace, I carry you about
in silent conversation, not a vulgar shout.

THE TRAUMA OF MY LIFE

The last words I heard Candace say, after I desperately kissed her on an emergency hospital visit, were "I love you too."

Then, a few hours later, her gaping-mouth profile was on view, after choking on her food killed her at the height of her chronic lung disease, bronchiectasis, ending our fifty-year marriage.

This traumatic event directed my grief-smothered next few days. I still haven't recovered.

I SOMEHOW CONNECT WITH HER

A dead person can be loved obliviously,
but the lover knows what he's doing.
He's preserving her essence
with his own effervescence.
He brings her back to remembered life
that he's well acquainted with.
He knows his own length and width,
which somehow she imaginarily fits.
He'd love to smother her with his mitts,
and as always, trade wits.
He loves her same as ever,
but she can't respond, never.
Still, I must forgive her,
since an imaginary spirit has to live her,
since our essences merge
to do what I urge,
even if only on the verge.
My grief will supply the power
to bring back some lost hour,
and make it somehow flower.

EPITAPH
MINUS PHOTOGRAPH

I'm my wife's mourner.
Death has torn her
from my intimate company,
so I'm unaccompanied
by her dear familiar self,
who resides on memory's shelf.
My heart is numb
and I'm struck dumb.
Her end was so abrupt
as to interrupt
our life's continuity,
full of fluidity.
All I have is grief,
without the benefit of relief.
So I turn over a new leaf
and submit to depression.
If only I had one more session
to proclaim my lonely obsession
and summon her from above
and play around with our pure love,
which is no longer there.
She smothered, having run out of air
for her chronic lung infection.
My love dwarfs mere affection,
burdened with ideal's perfection.

LAST WORDS, BUT NOT REPEATED

(ME:) Even though you're dead, can't you say again "I love you too" the way you did as your last words before choking to death from chronic lung disease?

(CANDACE:) No, I'm too dead to do that, so I'm forced to be as indifferent to you as to be to everyone else, now.

(ME:) But can't you make an exception for me?

(CANDACE:) No, it's against Death's rules. But be content that my exception would be there if I were allowed it.

A POIGNANT DIALOGUE

As a recent widower, I can't get relief from the grief which is virtually incessant. Candace is poignantly haunting me.

Eventually you'll have gone through grief's cycle. Your system will have absorbed it.

What's the difference between grief and mourning?

Both have to do with sorrow from the loss of a loved one. "Lament" is another attempted description.

Definitions can be cold and sappy. She's too dear for me to get over.

Stop sentimentalizing.

I'm too human. Candace and I were too human together.

Be realistic.

This *is* realism, however insipid that seems.

GOING ALONG

Life without Candace sadly proceeds,
and memory takes care of my needs
to have her with me at all times.
We can't hold hands, but otherwise
we're together if I mentally improvise,
as we walk the streets together
in varying sorts of weather,
and letting our minds have free play,
making comments across the way.
Occasionally I yield a tear
when in the grip of a different year.
At all times we're our only dear.

CANDACE AND I ARE STILL A COUPLE,
HER DEATH NULLIFIED BY OUR BEING SUPPLE

Loving Candace through life
has lingered in her strife
of having to lose her precious life.
She keeps up with me, pace for pace
knowing her ghostly place
in death's register as my companion
from life's skyscraper to death's canyon.
Side by side we remain in rhythm,
joining harmonies from deep within,
and luckily continuing our magical spin,
showing how love breaks through barriers,
her dead but me alive as joint carriers,
having come a long way from being mere marryers.

**TWO LIVES UNITED,
SO DON'T BE AFRIGHTED.
HERE ARE THEIR MYSTERIES
SOLVED BY THEIR HISTORIES**

When Candace and I first married,
I was older, but she died first
fifty years later
at the hospital, muttering
"I love you too."
Then her chronic lung disease
led to her decease
through horrible choking,
and I'm not joking.
But despite this, somehow
we remain together, and how!
My life and her death combined,
and here we are, entwined,
being overlapped by the same mind.
How did that actually occur?
We resumed the same rhythm where we were.
So here we are, together, me and her,
equipped with the same words to confer,
despite her death, lovingly to purr.
Surely this must give you a stir.

**BETWEEN HER DEATH AND MY LIFE,
I'M IN A KIND OF MENTAL STRIFE
IN A PUZZLE ABOUT MY WIFE**

Candace is dead, and I'm alive,
but our union must survive.
We ended so much together
that the difference between life and death
we managed to weather.
Does that sound mystical?
No. I mean it physical:
I take up her death's slack
by managing to get her back.
She's spiritually mine again,
overcoming difference between now and then,
as if her death now regained her life then.
Don't think I'm touched by insanity
to restore her life organically.
Am I taking an unholy liberty?
No, my mind isn't warped. I drink real tea.
Does that somehow reassure me?
No, I'm not going crazy.
It's just that my mind is sort of lazy.

LOVING CANDACE

Did I love Candace Watt?
Actually I still do, no matter what.
That was no figment of my imagination.
It was true blue, in the land of sensation.
Is she still available?
Not quite. She can't respond
in the sense that Britain is beyond the pond.
Is she inaccessible?
Maybe, but she's still blessable.
But this sounds too much like a confessable.
To be with Candace, nothing was wrong.
I wish I could set it to musical song.
To be with Candace was positively right.
I wish I could set it in front of my sight
to the full extent of shining light.
Let her be able to confront me
in real life that will shine,
so that she could still be mine,
and I could still be hers
without the defect of blurs
that I get from tears
that cover all those years.

SCARED

My death is coming.
I can't tell when.
I'm ninety-two and scared.
I have a heart problem
and sometimes feel faint.
I can't afford to fall.
If so, I may lose it all.
I just lost my beloved wife
of over fifty years.
How long can I stay
till the end of my long day
that was a whole lifetime?
When is my day of doom?
I'll lose the contents of my memory
to my old dreaded enemy.

WE'RE JOINED?
NOT REALLY

Goodbye, Candace, I join you in death,
sharing your recent loss of breath.
I already mourned for you,
and that's what I'm going through.
We'll be both two old-timers,
and I'm through with all my rhymers
that never awarded me fame.
So I'll join you with an irrelevant name
that was anonymous and now posthumous.
I loved you forever, but what about me?
What a euphemism to declare us "free"!

I'M FOLLOWING HER?

Candace, I'll die too
after mourning you.
Death will give my grief
no relief.
We'll be strictly apart
in death's anonymous art.
Your last words were "I love you too"
at your hospital.
Thank you for your tribute.
For a lonely while, it bore fruit.
I always loved you, my sweetest cute.
Now I finish up *route* route.

THAT TIME IS GONE
FOR ME TO DWELL UPON

(Belated Dialogue)

When I was with Candace all those years as my wife, I didn't fully appreciate her enough. I took her for granted. Now that she's dead, I realize how much I really miss her. This is called "belated appreciation," and puts me in the bad. I should have been more demonstrative in my appreciation, but her death makes it too late, and I feel remorse.

That's sad and tragic. How will you compensate?

I can't. It's too late.

Can you retrace your steps?

That's beyond my depth.

Loving someone who's dead is emotionally self-defeating. The dead one naturally remains helpless, and is of no use to anyone, especially not to the one who loves the current corpse. Life and death are in dysfunctional relationship, and are an unholy admixture. In reality, they shouldn't go near each other, but stay safely away and out of danger of touching. It's dirty and filthy business. The motto should be "to each its own." Strict segregation should be in effect. Keep categories unblemished in their enforced independence.

A QUICK DEPARTURE

The hospital did its best, but she was in such pain,
but without complaint.
Death was a sharp cut-off.
There was nothing left, not even a cough.
It opened up an irreducible margin
between Candace and Marvin.
Suddenly she was entirely lost.
Death accepted no answer.
It moved away, like a hurried dancer
with such haste
as to catch up with the performance
that started without her.
Now everything is without her
except only me.
Her death is barely started
for us to be so parted.
Here I'm holding grief
with no sign of relief.
But feel sorry for us both,
who both signed the troth
with a deep sigh of oath,
signifying former growth.

MORE THAN EVER

Loving Candace more than ever
now that she's dead—
is that a spiritual blessing?
It's certainly not a lessening.
Maybe it's a lesson.
Does it contain a message?
The revival of too many memories
haunts me as never before.
Why do they choose now to appear?
They only occur to *me*,
so I have a double burden
and have to bear her load,
or the inside of me will explode.
Does this contain a mystery code?

"JOIN ME!" IS MY HELPLESS PLEA

Being alone while she's dead
brings too many memories to my head,
which we can't share.
It hurts me to be so bare.
I need her to join,
representing the other side of the coin
which has two faces,
so the coin slides.
I need her sharing,
or I can't be bearing
being the sole representative
in our only active world
successfully unfurled.
Oh join me, Candace,
to spread our canvas.
You're the absent one
making me only half done.
We used to have such fun.
It can't be reproduced.
Neither of us can be seduced.
Being halves, we're reduced.
I'm too alone
and bruised to the bone.
I miss you too much,
especially your dear lovely touch.
Let's reminisce
for gossip we miss,
and meanwhile constantly kiss.
You're the part that's missing
for talking and listening
with dashing eyes glistening.

A FREE MAN

I'm a free man now that Candace is dead.
Free to love her more and more
right down to her inner core,
where my love has its great big store.
So many memories are released
in my unwelcome privacy
that her being absent is a piracy.
Why can't she join me at this?
It would contain too much bliss.
My having exclusive exposure
is too secret a disclosure.
She's as free as a bird,
being neither seen nor heard.
We're so unequal,
I'm yearning for a sequel
like a high-gliding mountain eagle
far away from the nest,
and it's not for the best.

**TOO DIVIDED,
OUR GAP WIDENED**

Between Candace and me,
I'm the only living one
who's taking advantage,
so I'm the expansive
one, free as a bird
who can be seen and heard,
while she's shut up in death's cage
and can't emerge.
She could be my companion
to roam the wide canyon,
but we're on different levels.
I'm one of the free devils.
She's helplessly out of commission;
and mine is a remembering mission—
for divided couples a tradition.

HOW WE DIFFER!

A dead woman is loved by a living man:
This is the pitiful epitome
of inequality
as a horrible policy.
I'm the one who's loving,
she being my beloved.
We're between two exposures
that go together like explosions.
What divided wills unite us!
I'm the one frightened,
being too enlightened.
She's mechanically dead
with an inoperable head
that doesn't respond
and can't correspond.
I'm the one who's fond
and sees her image in any pond.

WE'RE LIKE VIRTUAL STRANGERS.
BUT AT LEAST THERE ARE NO DANGERS

I spell it out clearly:
I love her dearly.
She's too dead to be loving.
We're total misfits
as far as phlegm can be spit,
or milk can be spilt.
We're former lovers in different states
like between night and day.
What a strange and weird couple
whose relationship is beyond being supple!
It's like we're from different species
of tribal disharmony.
I ask myself: what's the harm in me?
She's not self-critical,
so finds no fault
in being mixed with different elements, like salt.
At such odds, at least we don't assault.
Let our two selves find a form of peace
that varies widely from piece to piece
in our entire composition
of very mixed disposition.
We go on and find rapport
that opens every door.
Loving her takes effect,
so what else did you expect?
One dead and one alive.
And yet the mixture will survive.
Not only that, but even thrive.

WE WERE THE SPLIT VICTIMS OF OUR JOINT SYSTEMS

Everybody has to go through sorrow
and then try to forget it tomorrow.
My wife of so many years died,
and so automatically I cried.
So much love between us
had to be buried with such fuss
as suited a mourning ceremony,
making me intolerably lonely,
without being joined by Candace
while I toppled to the canvas.
The memories were crashing through my mind
to relentlessly remind.
They just couldn't be shared,
so I alone despaired,
and she even worse fared
by being seemingly spared.
Being both tragic,
there was no redemptive magic.

**CANDACE DIED.
I SURVIVED**

Death divorced Candace and me,
so now we're both free
from our successful love contract,
so we're out of contact.
But I love her still,
even though she's so still
as not to respond
when I wax so fond.
She's unable to reply,
but doesn't aim to defy.
Her last words at the hospital
were very responsible.
She said, "I love you too."
But then I cried and wept,
and my heart was utterly swept
with such love, there's no relief
for my devout grief.
My memories went overboard,
and ripped and roared,
too realistically restored.

I GOT A GLIMPSE!
BUT THAT WAS THE WORK OF IMPS

I dreamed that Candace rose from the dead
to reappear with her old body and head
that were momentarily animated
and virtually uncontaminated.
But it was too good to be true.
So once again she disappeared from view
and frustrated my living self
to rejoin her effigies back on the shelf
as though truly rejected
instead of lovingly expected.
What was real and what was not?
Ruling Death retied the old knot.
Thus my grief reappeared,
and all was left the way I had feared.
Was it a terrible tease?
It certainly wasn't designed to please.

**IMPOSSIBILITY
RUINS MY TRANQUILITY**

Since Candace has died,
she's always defied
my wish she'd return
to lovingly earn
the right to be mine again
the way she was, way back when.
But she remains rigid
like an immovable digit.
I can't get her loving soul
back in my clutches to love it whole.
Perhaps it wasn't in the books
to steal from the impossible like crooks.

FOR ETERNAL LOVE,
KEEP LOOKING ABOVE.
NEED HELP? I'LL GIVE YOU A SHOVE

When I started loving Candace,
when would it ever stop?
That was before marriage.
When would it ever stop?
Marriage lasted fifty years.
But when she dies, love disappears?
No, it's still here with me
kissing her soul that roams free.
I pursue her after her death,
and continue till my own last breath.
What remains is out of view
in the love still loyal for us two.
During all that interim, maybe it's still true.
It comes from out of us both
still honoring our original troth.
It's been so withstanding time,
is it ferociously still in its prime?
Will it last till I run out of rhyme?

**WE WERE OUTSMARTED
TO BE SO PARTED**

Where are you, Candace?
What does it mean to be dead?
Did it happen only to your head?
Or did it include your body too?
Have you only rotted
in the general scheme of being plotted?
Did it all come to nothing
and we can never share memories
that made us love each other?
Is our shared history
only a figment of mystery?
Are we denied of what happened
in real years together?
Am I the one holding the bag
while your part has fallen behind in lag,
so we can no longer play tag?

"CAUSE AND EFFECT"
CUT DOWN DEFECT

Why must I be turned into a grief machine
to add gasoline
to my loss of Candace?
For her, my days of mourning
occur at evening, afternoon, and morning.
Will I never be offered relief
from these days of incessant grief?
This has extended beyond belief.
All this, for whom?
Candace, the cause of my gloom.
She was my wifely sweetheart
from whom I couldn't bear to depart.
Hence I venture into this poetic art.

**OUR TWO SOULS
IN ONE ENROLLED**

Our two souls were living together
in all sorts of emotional weather.
Then what broke up our very tolerable tether?
Her death, what else?
In her, I had invested myself.
What am I without her?
Just a writing machine
on whom she pours gasoline
to make my car perpetually purr,
and our "two lives in one" occur.
But now she can't even stir,
while I greedily have energy
to make us permanent in our memory.

SEPARATED,
BUT EVER RELATED

When Candace died,
my eyes never dried.
The degree to which I care
makes her absence a nightmare.
She was light-colored and fair.
By love were we attached,
and didn't need to be evenly matched.
Far away she's gone, having been snatched.
I remain in life, she's gone to death,
and I miss her every breath.

**WORDS REPLACED BY TEARS
SUMMONED UP THOSE OLD YEARS**

When Candace died, my grief
was without relief.
We had so much to talk about
besides reviving old memories
in a methodical series
of reminiscences.
So silence assailed us both,
of which she wasn't aware,
being already dead,
so I was ahead,
and saw her so helpless
that I invaded her with my tears
to invoke all our old years.
The words that those tears replaced
were our final time we faced.
Since then there are more,
but without her presence.
But we achieved our essence
without animated effervescence.
We exchanged our blessings
with no discernible lessening,
but it was refreshing
to get her last emanation
from her exhausted heart.
Then it was time to depart,
like a last stroke in a work of art.

A MEMORY FROM THE GRAVE.
WHAT MUST I DO, BE BRAVE?

My former wife Candace is now a bundle of skull and bones.
She has thoughts from the grave, sent to me on loans,
provided I keep them secret,
or else she'll fill me with regret
that she didn't send them on the internet
for me to share them with my friends,
even though they're only composed of odds and ends.
What's so valuable of what she sent?
Full of intimacies here and there
that I wouldn't want the public to share.
They'd look at me with disbelief,
how wrenching has been my grief
to have lost Candace to the arms of Death
that deprived me of her loving breath.
It's so vastly beyond my depth
to discuss this matter any further.
She accuses Death of being responsible for her murder.
Thus I still beweep with tears
the loss of our memories of previous years
which only belong to me and my dear's.

TO MY DEAD WIFE

Let's remember together the times we went through,
and reminisce the details of every view
of gardens and restaurants and all of that,
which we shared in old times and about which we can chat.
We'll analyze the parties and social dinners,
and remember having been angels and sometimes sinners.
But we can't. You're dead and only I remember these things
which give nothing to you, but everything to me it brings.
Your silent voice is never within reach,
so I'm a chatterbox, and all I do is preach.
If only we can find items suitable to each!
Death does no good to the living,
so what in hell can the latter be giving?
The dead can't hear a blasted thing,
but the living are doomed to remember everything,
and even distort what's forgotten to the core,
because what good is a fact check any more?
Is accuracy all that reliable?
To burst into bitter tears I'm liable.

A REASSURING END

Candace's last words were "I love you too."
Of her it was my last view
in the impersonal hospital.
Was that possible?
It put a parting touch on our bond
to journey her off to the beyond.
"Infinity" was a superstition,
but put me in a rhapsodic position
to which to cling.
It had an eternal ring.

**HER LAST WORDS BEFORE SHE DIED
TO ME WERE "I LOVE YOU TOO"**

You can't take that away from me.
I hoard it for all eternity
as her life's last beckoning
deserving all later reckoning.
Now we're allied forever
past death, to keep us together.
I'm equipped with her message.
I'll use it as her essence,
as substitute for her presence,
who's my exceptional precious
to keep me company
as we enter the empty
and fill its bag with our plenty.
Over it, I'll stand sentry.

SOMEHOW TOGETHER

I loved Candace with all my heart,
but her death pushed us apart
after so many years of loving marriage,
keeping us in our own divine carriage.
Now we two are so silent,
it appears almost to be violent.
Our love will abstractly endure forever.
How could it separate us ever?
It must as usual be pure
to give me a sense that's absolutely sure.
My memory alone will keep in view
whatever or however we went through.
I lovingly retain it as tarnished but true.
At least I have just that version
to be singlemindedly converging.
I'll cover for her absence
to give me some abstract sense.
Then I'll have my Candace
with a camera that's candid.
She's the one I landed
to hold and hug forever
and never lose her ever.

**A HORRIBLE BLOW
BROUGHT ME DOWN LOW**

Candace died,
but I remained too alive
to join my departed wife.
I was lost without her.
My life was a dark blur.
What would I prefer?
That Candace revive
by her violating Death
and getting back her living breath
to rejoin me in the ranks
of life, and I profusely give her thanks.
Then we resume as before
to mutually adore.
But I'm requesting too much magic,
so our separated lives remain tragic.

OUR FINAL EXCHANGE
INDICATED NO ETERNAL CHANGE

Candace said "I love you too"
as her last words.
That was all the glory I needed.
In my miserable happiness I heeded:
Those loving words of tribute
that embellished our bond, which was a beaut
which convince eternity we were fond.
You can never take it away from me
if we still that way agree.
We have each other's words
that never tossed lightly were any absurds.

"HELLO, BUN"

My darling Candace has died.
I dreamed of her and cried.
She said, "Hello, Bun."
I'm still in a state of stun.
She was miserable from her lung disease
which was to lead to her decease.
All that we had shared
when we were paired,
of trips and friends and places,
where we could see each other's faces,
we had intended to review
as if miraculously to renew.
I knew her right down to her core,
and was ready to remember more.
But she could no longer function
when the pain punctured her sleep.
All I could do was silently weep
when her darling life she couldn't manage to keep.
I sobbed to think of her current state
to divide horribly our joint fate,
when that cute little thing was my mate.
She took care of me with money
as my protective honey.
Why can't we continue to hug
in my old role as her loving lug,
when we matched up our genders
and aligned their respective splendors
before they only became sorrowful lenders?

THE SUBJECT OF MY DREAMS
IS STILL SUFFERING, IT SEEMS

I once again dreamed of Candace
on my screen's well-painted canvas.
Predictably, I again cried,
because she had recently died.
She was my wife who fled,
when all the blood in my heart bled.
I had loved her with all my heart
only to see the two of us part
on my visit to the hospital,
which I knew was eminently possible.
Now I can never reclaim her.
Useless to pity me or blame her.
Only in dreams can she reappear.
Should I welcome her image, or fear?
I dread to break down in sobs,
because Candace has joined Death's rowdy mobs
in their unruly promiscuity.
What's she doing with those throngs
she finds herself amongs?
Oh Candace, I loved you too much
not to die myself for your precious touch.

A LETTER TO CANDACE

Part of my mind must be assuming that somehow you're still alive, so I'm not being realistic by writing to you, which is based on false pretense. I still somehow feel your "being" as close to mine. We had so many joint experiences together, seeing the same people together, and the same flowers on Botanic Garden paths, and shopping, and eating. I feel your being. You escaped from your horrible lungs and throat sufferings. The hospital was about to send you to a hospice for morphine to relieve you. We went through so much together. I still feel your closeness, despite your new category as formerly rather than presently alive. You're still with me. But you can't read or talk or write. I'm fooling myself in order to stop crying, or to prevent a new outburst of tears—yours or mine?

IN GRIEF
BEYOND BELIEF

What a brief brevity!
But we had some fun and levity
when you were able to live with me,
till you were punched out on the canvas,
so goodbye to my dear Candace.
You were my perfect wife
so long as we shared life.
I was hoping for more
till departure from the one I adore.
What does it feel to be dead?
Has it gone to your sweet head?

LOVING CANDACE

WHAT A BREAK!
WITH SO MUCH AT STAKE!

Candace Watt being my wife
was the best break in my life.
She steered me in the right direction
and put on it her special inflection
that bears research and reflection.
So thank you, my dear Candace,
for depicting me on the right canvas.
I'll search for your soul all the way to Kansas.

WHEN CANDACE DIED

When Candace died,
I was well supplied
in grief and mourning
from night to afternoon to morning.
She was my eternity
until her infirmity,
then afterward too
so long as I could pursue
in the presence of that double view.

OUR LOSS

When I was given birth
on this big round earth,
who knew how long I could stay
to be able to do work and play?
But when I met Candace Watt,
don't ask me "What?"
She settled my fate for good,
and we lived in the same neighborhood.
Therefore our alliance stood
till the very end—
a tragedy that I couldn't mend.

WRITTEN IN PROSE
FOR ALL THOSE

Candace died, but how can I stop loving her? When I recall our multiple times together, my eyes have tears, as if in commemoration of those years. It's like her soul is connected with mine. She's in my company constantly, with periodical interruptions. Then why do I feel lonely? Because she's my only. So am I unfaithful with all the other invisible others? They're temporary Candace-substitutes. I fill in their invisibilities to the best of my imaginative abilities. Thus I'm a Don Juan. That's why I'm so pale and wan. I tell the others not to be envious or jealous, which are two words that buzz around each other like twins. Which one wins?

THE HOSPITAL

I loved Candace with all my might
and was glad to see her sight.
Many a smile passed between us
whenever we would come and go.
She was sometimes a gloomy soul,
so I rallied her to cheer.
The main thing was that we were near.
But then she died from her rotten disease.
My love and mourning would never cease.
My eyes are moist when I think
back to our wedding, and now the lonely link.
How could we be without each other?
How was that at all possible?
I cherish our last meeting in the hospital.
Frantically was how I kissed her
before the sorrow set in to miss her.

BEING CLOSE

Being without Candace for the rest of my life
I'll get used to, as a plight.
But I always innerly weep
when from her I have a clean sweep
while her dream image riots in my sleep.
The two of us run very deep.
But the course of nature will not let us keep.
I now think her as only herself
without the need for me to help.
Yet there will be the occasional tear
to envisage us together as being near.

WHEN CANDACE LEFT, I WAS BEYOND BEREFT

In remembering Candace,
I get good and frantic,
for when she died she gave me panic
enough to feel so antic.
My love for her was defeated
when her dreadful death depleted
my wish to have many more years
with her beyond our tears,
having realized our ultimate fears.
So she's not "there" any more,
the only one I can adore.
I still live in the land of life.
Without her, it's continual strife.
Why must I keep longing
for her where she's no longer belonging?
Of course it makes no sense
that forgetting her I can't dispense,
even in self-defense.
My mourning is immense.
Is death such an adversary
as to be worse than unnecessary,
to deprive me of ever being merry
when they plow her down to bury?
Do I miss her? Oh, not very!

WHAT YOU'VE SACRIFICIALLY DONE FOR ME BY MAKING ME PRODUCTIVELY FREE

I remember the wondrous deeds that Candace did for me and us both
with her workmanlike doses of generosity.
She did so much self-sacrifice for my benefit,
with her having fun too.
I'm indebted to her beyond her grave
for liberating me from drudgery to grant me free time
to proceed with developing my writing career.
She enlarged my fields of opportunity,
working hard at her daily full-time office job,
while I, as her grateful parasite,
took her generosity's full advantage
with freedom to ponder and produce literature
and bask in endless activity at permissive leisure.
She was my truly loving wife
who enabled my bountiful life.
If only I could tell her now,
but my sweet dear is in skeletonic clothes,
and her large-hearted giving capacity is closed.
Thanks for indulging my being your recipient
that has so empowered me to come into my own
by catching the rescue mechanism you have thrown.
Thanks for supporting me,
and constantly rewarding me.
I hope I gave something back
so we could have equal track.

NOT GETTING WHAT YOU WANT
IS A VERY COMMON STUNT

Communicating is what I used to get from and give to my now
    dead wife.
It was the crucial ingredient of verbal exchange.
What we used to want and now can't get
is life's big lost bet.
In most cases we learn to do without,
if you can't get what you want.
In this case I suffer grief
and do without relief.
Being in love is to be spoiled.
You want a new dose of what you can't do without,
so that's what a "broken heart" is about.
I can't unlearn it or adapt or adjust.
Therefore a "broken heart" is just not just.
Philosophy can't control
my simply playing my role.
It's too serious to be droll.
Basic and elementary
are the big wants of the century.
"If you can't get what you want, stop wanting"
is a hard nut to be confronting.
No use going around grunting.

LOVE IS ALL THAT REMAINS
OF THESE INERADICABLE STAINS

I've never been so sad in my life,
having lost my darling wife.
I went to kiss her in the hospitable,
because visiting her was still possible.
Nurse told me she choked on her food.
The cleaned up corpse was brought before me
on a special table.
To stop staring I wasn't able,
though I wanted to look away.
Her jaws were bound apart,
and not another word could be spoken
after my murdered heart was already broken.
We had planned to reminisce about the past.
That was, of course, assuming she would last,
and we were planning to have a blast
renewing recollection and memory,
not reckoning death our enemy.
Of what we shared all those years,
now she's dead and I'm in tears.
That's one way of being apart.
Is there another, in all of art?
Well, that will do for a start.

**EVERYTHING IS SHARED
AND NOTHING IS SPARED**

My eyes are a constant downfall of tears
now that I've lost my wife after many years.
She taught me the meaning of love,
which is a great gift from above.
My wife was mine. She belonged to me,
but she's now been set "free,"
which she never longed to be.
To be with me was her goal.
To be with her was my role.
We neither had complete control.
The world separated us, from pole to pole.
But by it we were ignited
to remain forever united,
although now needless to be sighted.
By cruel death were we slighted.
By her, the world's light blew out
to be forever in shade throughout.
How dim that her radiance is in doubt.
In dismal voice I emit a shout
that doesn't boast of any clout.

SHE AND I
TOGETHER.
IN THE BACKGROUND IS THE SKY.
THAT'S OUR PORTRAIT
AND OUR DEFENSIVE FORTRESS

All I can be is humble,
and that's how I mumble,
now that Candace is out of the picture,
but flung back in with elixir.
I love her for us,
but death took her away,
so I miss her every day.
"Here today and gone tomorrow"
is a capsule summary of my sorrow.
How sweet-hearted and lovely she was
to create the inner confines of our buzz
along with me, her mate,
who hereby pronounces her as "great."
We did it ourselves. Don't call it fate.

MONEYBAG, SO MY WRITING DIDN'T LAG

(1)

She gave me support
with her salary's income. What a sport!
That's my good report.
Against poverty, she protected my fort.
That's her, the generous sort.

(2)

Loving Candace is taken for granted.
That's how it was planted.
Is she thoroughly deserving?
Yes, because she was serving
me as my financial supporter,
otherwise, how could I afford it
to have enough leisure to write
and thus take a big bite
of literary esteem,
with a full head of steam?
Candace was like a dream
that came to occupy the real world
with her full generosity unfurled.
Where would I be without her,
who gave my writing a powerful stir?
She was more than OK, sir.

SHE SUPPORTED ME WITH A WELL-EARNED SALARY.
SO FOR RHYME'S SAKE, SHE COULD BE NAMED VALERY

Candace was a fighter,
so she fought for me as a writer.
She believed my writing was worth it,
so she helped give birth to it.
Her money allowed me not to be employed
except for literature's sophisticated joys
for my special work of choice.
She helped me make
a career, many books published,
but only for the literary public.
So I was a special taste
that Candace determined must never go to waste,
so the fruits of my labor were well placed.
She was the best lucky break that I faced.
She inspired such love
that where could it be born except exquisitely above,
like the uncaged fluttering dove
from his mother's nest
high above the rest?

WE DID EACH OTHER GOOD
IN THE SAME NEIGHBORHOOD

A tale of good cheer:
My literary career
was mainly financed by Candace's salary.
She paid for all the vegetables, including celery.
So I thanked her with all my heart
that Candace's earnings played a large part
in prolonging my auspicious start
in the charmed poetic art.
Candace and I became a loving pair,
unlike some couples who are neither there.
And she treated me so square
that she paid for the rent,
being heaven sent,
and for all the food
to keep me in the poetic mood.
So that's where we stood.
For both of us, it was for the good.
We couldn't love each other more
from our joint loving core.
We knew what each other were for,
and were determined to do and be it more.
What we did was mutually adore,
so love in heaven continued to soar,
and both of us racked up the score,
which was much higher than before.

**GOING DEEP
IN BEING CHEAP**

I was Candace's parasite,
so I leeched and sponged off her,
and got away, scot free,
with so many unpaid benefits
that it amounted to a huge profit
on all sides of the self-help zone
whose motto is "to each his own,"
right down to the bone.
I was known for being very cheap,
to the extent of avoiding paying.
A sheer delight was to save money
by giving the excess to my honey—
Candace, who kissed me as reward,
calling me "money's stingiest lord,"
which was the limit I could afford.
Oh, how the two of us mutually adored,
once we had our combined money restored!
A financial expert we consulted
told us how it all resulted
without needing to be insulted.

SHE SUFFERED AND DIED

So many memories are chased
by thoughts of Candace, when we raced
together in taxis to your doctors.
We shared being together
to your psychoanalyst and elsewhere,
and then to sweet home together
after buying food for dinner
which you prepared with your skill,
and all those times you were fighting being ill,
and the pains from your diseases
were building up steadily.
Finally we had to hire home health aides' help,
and the doom was cast.
You suffered day and night,
but I had you and you had me.
Oh my darling, how could you die and leave me?

FIGHTING PAIN AND DISTRESS
ON SO MANY TAXIS

Candace kept on suffering,
and I had to witness all that.
She always seemed to be ill,
as if almost by will,
and I chased along
in so many taxis
through painful years.
We were fighting your constant pain,
but shared the distress.
I would be alongside
for us to share every ride,
till you had to subside.
Now I miss you so terribly.
For you, it went perishably.
Now you fell into death,
and I miss breathing your breath
that was hectic while we chased.
Such seemed always the case
while tears rolled down my face.

CANDACE'S EFFECT

After my wife died,
I loved her more than ever
because of nostalgia and grief,
which were beyond belief.
I craved to relive the old scenes
that linked us together as a pair.
We went here, we went there,
and I never got over them
when they took on her charm,
which had the power to disarm
me to the point of alarm.
She had a certain magic,
so to lose her was tragic,
and also made me nostalgic
for whatever occurred in the past,
built and designed to last.
The time went by too fast.
But now it's too slow,
because she's only below
with nowhere else to go.
She's so solitary,
who used to smile and make merry.

**CANDACE AND SNOW
CREATE GREAT WOE**

After many years, snow fell
in New York City,
pronounced very pretty.
I used to share it with Candace
from windows and outside.
But now she's died.
That's part of our memory
that we can't share,
because she's not there.
Precisely, that's what I can't bear.
It just doesn't seem at all fair!
How could it happen to me—
this horror that I can't flee?
The snow is gone that we used to share.
She's also gone, whom I can't share.
That's my life's curse,
there being no worse.
She can't be by my side
with her nose red due to Winter cold,
and I beside her, proud and bold.
This tale is dismally told
while I collapse and fold
without her to comfort and hold.

LOVING CANDACE

**LIFE WITH HER I CAN'T SHARE.
THAT'S THE RESPONSIBILITY I BEAR**

Your brain is out of whack
because you can't get Candace back.
Her death is your acute lack,
so you pour out endless grief,
and are starved for relief.
So that's your state of being:
your being deprived of seeing
her familiar face.
That's the thing you can't face.
It haunts you all the time
as punishment for love's crime.
You're horribly guilty
and feel responsibly filthy.
It bears down, soon to wilt me,
a burden I can't flee.

**LOSSES
ARE YOUR BOSSES.
FIND OUT WHAT CAUSES**

To lose life is to lose your best friend,
which is the very end.
Can anything make amend?
To lose Candace is to lose love,
than which nothing is above.
My life is gone to pieces,
since Candace has deceased
due to physical disease.
I lose the love of my life.
Can I bear this utmost strife?
Obviously, no.
Such is the source of my woe.
Can there be a worst
to sum up how I'm cursed?
Of all evils, that comes first,
if bearing sufficient intensity
commensurate to that immensity.

I MET HER AS A MISS, AND MADE HER A MISSUS

Candace is the one I miss.
She might have remained a Miss,
but I made her into a Missus
by legally marrying
after a bit of tarrying.
Was she still a Missus after she died?
I'm fit to be tied.
What are the rules
that are our social tools?
She represented to me "Love."
Is there anything in the world above?
Not for me.
Pardon while I weep,
as she invades my sleep
from out of the deep.
Weeping is my only resort
other than this heartful report,
to which she can't retort.
Meanwhile, how can I hold the fort?
I'm waiting for etiquette to have me taught
if there's anything of the sort.
Thus my weeping ends with a laugh,
so I divide them in half,
and go crazily daft.

OF FRIENDS AND OTHER MEMORIES

On July 8, 2017 Marvin Cohen wrote:

the other side of death is laughter, gaiety, & rejoicing.

WHAT I SEEM TO HAVE SEEN

Oh my dead friends are passing by
in memory's long parade,
crossing Fifth Avenue on to Broadway
and on London's murky streets,
in their usual finery they were clothed by,
marching in short strides and long uneven steps
with masklike faces familiar yet strange too,
wraithlike, ghouls, yet preserved anew,
reaching for my moods, blowing old tunes
on winds whirling through my head
with their ears matching mine, the rhythms we loved together.
Death holds them fast, and keeps me loose away
to catch what views penetrate my living skull
gorging on them all, in the strain aghast
to haul them all in, to this uneven blast
of me as spectator, and them stuck too solidly in their lost past
I seem to see again, but now my vision melts,
and the parade's last step has stepped away
from a platform on mentality's staggering stage.

PHILOSOPHICAL WAGERS
WE'VE DEBATED FOR AGES

Memories are recorders of the past.
The possibilities are vast.
With such a lot to recall,
it's hard to preserve them all.
Which will fit the present's need?
Those are the reminders that we heed.
The human race is a selective breed.
What we remember at the right time
determines if we win or lose our dime.
So figure things out, but take your time,
or else hurry before we run out of time.
So many things are too late
as to make precarious our notions of fate.
Sometimes it's best to just stand and wait.
Better not to carry too much freight.
Ah, to make the right decision
deals with the roundabout more than precision.
So introduce anarchy into life,
along with that item of juicy strife
that allows for the element of chance
to make life an enduring romance.
But many people end on a bad note.
Let's turn away and not give them our vote.
Yet there must be room for pity
in this realm of the ironic witty.

OUR RENEWED FRIENDSHIP SAILS ON AN UNSINKABLE SHIP, THAT ONLY TILTS AT ITS PORTSIDE TIP

I insulted my friend
without making an amend
of polite apology
from a gentleman's anthology.
Now I'll make recompense
if I had an iota of sense.
My friend soon forgave me.
Wasn't that sharp of brave me?
Now our friendship is renewed,
having been doubly reviewed.
All is warm and acute,
for my apology bore fruit.
He no longer calls me a brute,
and I've deftly avoided a suit.
He and I are now such pals
that now we jointly hunt pretty gals,
but sometimes argue,
since our renewed friendship is not made of glue.
Instead, it's made of paste,
so our renewal won't go to waste.
Thus, being patched here and there,
our new pact is granted a dose of air
that pumps us up full of flair.

DIALOGUE OF INEVITABLE SEQUENCE

Does memory come first?

On the contrary, it comes *after* what it's based on.

What is it based on?

Happenings, occurrences, events, experiences.

Those real-life-in-the-world things are what memory is based on and derived from?

Yes, in precise sequence.

So memory is a learning experience, teaching us a lesson?

Sure. Take advantage of that innate function.

But wouldn't that be exploitation?

In a good, necessary way, not harmful.

Then I'll continue as I was, without guilt.

Feel free to indulge your natural rights.

That I will, but I won't abuse them.

If you do, learn your penalties.

With all this information, I'll burst.

Burst in such a way as to bring yourself back in order again.

You've given me something to remember.

REVIVALS

The good old days, when you drove me around
in your ever trusty car,
have gone away so far
as to be lost to recollection,
seemingly not part of my collection.
My memory is so strained
that fewer and fewer images are retained.
Soon the past will be totally blocked out.
Re-entry will be so forbidden
as to be virtually hidden.
So please remind me, now and then,
what happened, and when.
Then I'll enjoy them all over again.
My head will be their repository
to revive all the elements of their story.
Some were of no consequence, but others had glory.

INVESTIGATING THE PAST
AND SLIGHTLY RENEWING ITS BLAST

(1)

Memory is a great device
that's practically without price.
It resides within my head,
allowing me to get ahead
of what's already happened, far away.
It brings back the light of another day
that gives my eyes a workout
so luminous, it's without doubt.
Even spectacles are not needed
for all this past to be regreeted.
Hello, Past. Now that we've re-met,
bring back some aspects of you that I don't regret.
Now that we're re-acquainted, aren't we all set?

(2)

You're like a dear old house once lived in,
once relinquished, but now I don't have to give in,
but simply let me reach back and re-win.
I'll ask that old house, "How have you been?
Who are your current residents?
They're part of my precedence.
Can you provide me their evidence?
Introduce us for what we have in common.
But let it be light, not solemn.
We'll take it all in stride,
this place where we reside.
It's like the earth itself.
Let's examine an inside shelf

and see what it contains
among the many remains.
They belonged to me and you.
Either one, it's equally true."

SHOULD WE BE DEPRIVED OF ANY SEASON WITHIN THE TRIAL OF HUMAN REASON?

When December arrives, twigs have lost leaves,
so Autumn's season leaves,
while colorful Fall's fan grieves.
Soon it will be New Year's Eve,
when to the tune of Robert Burns,
everybody's heart yearns
to remember old friends,
for some of whom, life ends.
Tears sprinkle from everyone's eyes,
since we all know how time flies,
while the Winter has long to go
before Spring melts the delicate whiteness of snow.
Thus, season to season, all will flow,
as the harsh early Spring's winds blow,
and dear old friends lie buried below.
Nostalgia is here to stay,
to remember back the other day.

IN REFERENCE TO ROBERT BURNS AT THE TIME THE YEAR TURNS

Let's raise a cup of kindness
to the memory of old friends.
It gives a warm glow to my heart
to recall the friends who had to depart.
How sad that they don't exist.
But memory makes them persist.
One day my memory will fail.
Away and away my doting heart will sail.
Our generation is not for long.
In its honor, let's sing Robert Burns' song
on New Years' Eve—what better time?
Here it is now. Ring the chime.
Let a tear drop drop.
From your eyelid it will pop.
Gravity will not let it stop.
The gravity of the occasion
speaks for its persuasion.
Nostalgia rules the eve,
and lets loose our common grieve.

MEMORY'S FIXED AUTOMATIC SEQUENCE IN THE BRAIN AS A COPY MACHINE

Can I ever remember something *before* experiencing it?

Never. The memory is *based* on the experience, which must *precede* the memory.

Good. If that's the nature of the brain, who am I to violate it?

It's not your choice. It's a one-way route or process or sequence. First go around the block and enter the world; then you've picked up your future memories by way of time's orderly procedure.

"First things first"?

Don't confuse it with "Safety First," which is basically a caution warning for preventing bad things from happening.

OLD FRIENDS

My old friends I still love,
the ones whom Death denied me of,
and the ones still very much alive.
On both those types my love will thrive,
and be the victim of "deprive."
My old friends I still love,
and continue to seek far above,
as the permanent emblems of my love?
Not as symbols, but just for themselves.
Into all those, my heart still delves.

MY MEMORY ENDOWMENT

I'll gather all my random memories
of dear old friends or dubious enemies,
that go way back to childhood and before,
or even recent, to collect all that lore.
It's like a running film or continual book:
the ones who happily recalled me, or forsook.
So many people crowded my life,
in harmonious times or those of strife.
I'm so glad I have no amnesia,
which would prevent memory from working easier.

ANOTHER VISIT

Remembering friends is all I do
as I float to death on the old canoe.
Why not be in their imaginary company
to pay still another longing tribute,
which has no purpose but ancient nostalgia,
which is of course self-defeating
like a bunch of sheep doing aimless bleating?
It's a wooly way of passing the time
devoted to loved ones in the ritual of death's crime.
Idly back and forth they come to me.
This is the contact I'm limited to,
trapped in the pressure of joining them
for the extra time that life will afford
to once again be on board.

THE PAST IS OUR PLAYTHING.
BUT IT'S NOT ALWAYS A GAY THING.
SOMETIMES IT'S TOO SAD
TO KEEP OUT THE BAD

The past is something you play with,
to revive or stay with.
Nostalgia is flexible to fool around with,
since it's yours to manipulate.
It's a matter of how we relate,
and to what or whom.
We could be there like a zoom.
We carry the past with us
like a mental barrier or passage.
We're walking museums
that have become mausoleums.
The past is buried right in our heads,
just next door to our death beds.
We keep it alive for a time
while still accessible is our rhyme.
Finally we pay death dues for our crime
of playing fast and loose with the burden of time.
It's all so very personal
and awaits passage to our burial
where we wave and shout merry all.

NOT QUITE RIGHT, THOUGH BEING OFF IS ONLY SLIGHT

Memory is a chaotic distorter
instead of an accurate reporter.
Its collection is currently in disrepair,
driving the recollector to despair
for presiding over a jungle-like gallery
whose hired attendants deserve no salary.
I confuse various old friends' images.
Possibly insanity is the guiding force.
I'm always slightly somewhat off course,
but "slightly" can lead to momentous,
like a peaceful valley becoming mountainly disordered.
It's like your income tax having to be audited,
and your whole integrity in question,
or a stomach's food-tumbling indigestion.
Soon I'll make my life so neat
that its immaculate symmetry is a treat,
although right now that's an impossible feat.
If visitors arrive, I'm at a loss how to greet.
Though there's no chair, should I ask them to have a seat?

WHAT YOU REMEMBER
AS A TRIBAL HUMAN MEMBER

Memory makes the past come alive,
but only as a duplicate print,
so it barely only gives a hint
of the deep and varied richness
in its pageantry.
The past itself is transferable
to the very present day,
but just as a matter of play.
Where you are now is like a film,
and I was the careless director
as well as the belated inspector.
So it's only a spectre?
In general it's no distortion.
All the visual elements are in proportion.
You get a fair picture
of your mind's depicture.
Some survive as a fixture.
So does memory overall do the job?
It catches what the past chooses to lob.
It's individual, not shared by the mob.
So when you get a contribution from the past,
exclaim with gratitude "At last!"
Each memory is a personal matter,
but sometimes shared with others as grist for chatter.
Memory comes in social use,
but you can bore others if you're obtuse
and let your conversation wander too loose,
sometimes out of context,
making bored listeners vexed,
hearing too much of your continual text.

MEMORY'S SEQUENCE LAW, INVENTED BY NATURE WITHOUT MIRACULOUS INTERVENTION

Could I ever violate the inviolable memory sequence law?

No, but what is it?

That you can't remember something unless you've first experienced it as a personal event or occurrence.

Impossible to reverse the order of that sequence: Experience it in the first place for it to be inside you to make remembering it possible. You have to first receive the original impression in your own brain for the memory to take its turn as potential latency.

Life is a laboratory where this never fails. You can try it yourself, immediately or eventually.

If it works on me, it works on everyone else under the rules of universal logic.

Try it. Be your own guinea pig in life's open laboratory for scientific amateurs.

Should I be honest about the result?

Therein lies the test of the experimenter's impeccable integrity. The scientific method forbids miracle, because it uses time as its proving ground.

I have grounds for believing you. But is there any occult magic in this?

No. It's "true-blue."

Good. I'm my own Galileo, Copernicus, Edison, Pasteur, or any other historical success worker on an incorruptible level.

Good. I wouldn't want a funny, peculiar accident to happen.

No. It must be orthodoxically kosher. Memory doesn't fool around. It's become its own law, with a legitimate self-judge and jury.

No rushing to justice, like in cowboy movies where a mob tries to lynch you?

Time has to prove itself.

You're a great advertising salesmanship, in addition to an impartial justice provider, under impeccable workmanship.

Thank you for those true compliments. I rest vindicated, even though never challenged.

PLAGUED BY UNWANTED MEMORY, AS IF BEGOTTEN BY YOUR WORST ENEMY

What you experienced created a potential memory
that forgetfulness may not protect you from.
With every occurrence or event,
memory may repeat in consequence.
So whatever happens to you is double,
plaguing you with more trouble.
Sometimes memories are nightmares
that give you nothing but despairs.
Experience has warped your brain
with what unwanted memory will sustain.
Voluntarily you want to forget,
so be careful of what experiences you'll beget
to be turned hideously into regret.

THE PAIL, BEARING SAND ALONG THE SHORE'S LAND

When I think back to my old friends,
all of whom met normal ends
in obedience to Death's command,
I think of life as a pail of sand
along the ocean's floor,
right at the border of the shore.
The pail soon shrinks of its load
of its grains of sand,
given up to the near-by land
as the wind freely blows.
That's how human life gradually goes.
Those old friends come to memory again,
and I feel chilly from the difference of now and then.
They were so gay and friendly,
that the empty pail mocks Death's careless entry,
that scatters to the wind those grains of sand,
in deferential obedience to Death's command
across the grim currents of the rented land.
The waves along the ocean splash.
To draw a metaphoric conclusion is rash.

**SAYING GOODBYE TO YOUR FAVORITE FRIEND
AT THE POIGNANT VERY END,
WITH THE BEST WISHES I COULD SEND**

My hoping your life has no end
is your reward for having me as friend.
Any old disagreements have already met amend.
Now that I'm about to die, I wish you well,
and well speeded to anywhere except hell.
I wish I could follow you about.
But death is my next step
to trip over.
I truly wish my life I could do over,
with you central in it.
Sorry, I have to leave this minute.
Having you as my friend
consoles me at my life's end.

ALONE OR TOGETHER
IS YOUR ALTERNATE SOCIAL WEATHER

It's great to be solitary,
but also to have company.
You can't have both at the same time.
So alternate, in your doubled life,
between being alone on the one hand,
and being together, which is also grand.
Being alone, you talk to yourself.
And with others, you lend out your self.
Both ways are fortifying,
to keep your spirits alternately flying.
With others you're complying.
But death is solitary when you're dying,
though sometimes it's assisted
by people whom you've never resisted,
when volunteered or requested.
But sometimes you're pestered,
and ask to be sequestered.
Even when with others, you need privacy
from the outer ranges of society,
which is composed of bewildering variety
that you have to sift among
to narrow down the throng
to those with whom you get along
and virtually sing the same song
with the same unified voice,
making just about the same choice.
If so happens, then rejoice.
Having a close friend
helps all your troubles to mend.
That person is there, to attend.

OF FRIENDS AND OTHER MEMORIES

Having a few of those
is better than none, I suppose.
They allow you to be altruistic,
so together you must all stick.
For a favorite, have your pick.

THOSE GOLDEN DAYS OF YOUTH
MADE US WONDER: WHAT WAS TRUTH?
WERE WE ALWAYS THAT UNCOUTH?

The clock is moving too fast,
so how long will I last?
I'm thinking nostalgically of my past
that was so full of youth
that it even exaggerated its own truth
to make it extra realistic,
such as the scarlet lipstick
that my girlfriend proudly wore.
When we kissed, it got stuck on my face,
and our lips glued together.
That was typical adolescent weather.
Her parents finally separated us,
but I was a laughing stock
whom my athletic friends would mock.
I couldn't fight back because they were stronger.
I wish my youth had lasted longer.
But too much nostalgia couldn't be wronger.
It makes me impatient with now,
with old age sprawled on my wrinkled brow.
But I loved life in those deeply felt days—and how!
Most of my friends are gone
into some or other sad beyond.
Sometimes we tried fishing in the pond.
Now my tears are beginning to fall
when I remember my friends—all.

**MEMORY
NEEDN'T BE YOUR ENEMY**

Whatever happened to you in the past,
thanks to candid memory, is able to last.
It can't get away too fast.
So memory is a preservative
that presents what can relive.
What a bouquet to give!
It's a marvelous gift
you can record with thrift
as an almost lifelong lift.
If you can avoid amnesia,
this process is even easier.

REJECTING MEMORY

How can I turn back the clock and be young again?

You can't. Not only is it unrealistic, it's even impossible.

Don't make fun. I'm in real agony. Being this old is no picnic. Or if it is, it's rained upon.

I have a helpful suggestion.

Please tell.

You can't go back with the clock's help, but with memories'. You have a whole youth to be nostalgic about, through memory's courtesy.

It would only help to shed tears. I can't revive those golden years. It would give me a mental breakdown to compare such archaic youth to my being in my nineties.

I'm sorry. Keep your sanity.

Along with my vanity, that makes me unique.

I'll treat you as such, not like you're a freak.

Just slightly oblique.

Keep your flesh intact, so you won't creak.

MEMORY GUIDE, BOTH FAR AND WIDE

Is it ever possible to remember things before you experience the events that you afterwards recall?

No. It's a strict sequence by rule. Memory is based on your first experiencing the corresponding event that then goes into your head as an immediate or potential memory.

It's not a rule of thumb, but a rule of head?

That's it. Now you're ahead of it.

I wouldn't carry it on my behind, unless maybe I sit on it. How will I remember this lesson?

Because I first told you.

Can you sometimes remember too much?

Yes, the mistakes you made, by regret. First you get. Then you forget.

Is there a way of making it easier?

Yes. By remembering not to have amnesia.

OH MY DEAR PAST!
WHY COULDN'T IT LAST?

Here today and gone tomorrow
brings a certain sorrow
as I sit lonely by the window
remembering good old times with friends
who have now met their ends.
We got too old to continue to play
that lovely old game of baseball
from the early Spring to the late Fall.
We had our jobs, but saw each other,
each a brother to the other.
Wedding bells tore us apart,
when baby making became an art.
But I'll never forget our wonderful start
nor the doom of having to part.
My memory is cluttered with old friends
with whom complete nostalgia contends.
Melancholy is their replacement
as I complete my stumble to the basement.

WHAT YOU CAN BUILD UP FOR LATER LIFE'S RECALL. INSTALL THEM UP AND YOU CAN HAVE THEM ALL

When you're suffering from memory loss,
be your own memory boss.
Have new experiences and events
to try out different memory extents.
So your brain will be full of new stuff
to recall freshly from the start
by building a new memory bank,
which later on you'll thank,
in which you invest dividends
and make some profits at the end.
So go out and about
by taking a series of tours
that will become all yours.
Travel will produce results
to enrich your lives as adults.
Do you have the means to afford them?
Then go aboard them,
whether near-by or abroad.
Experience the vast,
and they're yours later with a blast.
Hurry up, do it fast.
Life will not long wait
to produce your own fate,
whether sooner or late.
Is time itself the bait?

BEING DROPPED, LIKE SOMETHING SUDDENLY POPPED

I was dropped by my friend
who put our friendship to an end
abruptly without warning
and without an excuse.
Had I been guilty of abuse
of his delicate sensibility?
He had both sense and ability,
and so did I.
We were on an equal basis,
and looked in each other's faces
from the distance of a few paces.
We seemed to see eye to eye
from the perspective of the same sky.
What had taken place
that made him put away his face
from my long-familiar view?
There was no argument to be had
of an overt caliber.
We were always on each other's calendar,
and took familiar liberties
just to mainly tease.
Why are we no longer at ease?
Will someone tell me, please?

WHAT WILL HAPPEN IN MEMORY TO EVENTS YOU ONCE EXPERIENCED?

Once something happened,
memory may renew it.
If heartless, it may say "Screw it!"
Is the past a waste garbage dump
that may leave in our throat a lump?
Or is it such a blast
that renews itself and will last?
Hard to tell what will happen
to a potential renewal,
if time should revert to refusal.
It's worth our mystery perusal,
or doggedly pursuing the usual,
or mistakenly confounding the confusual.
Memory ought to be rewarding
after so much forwarding.
Maybe it reverts to its long lost past
with an apology that it didn't last,
having to sift through the vast?
It depends on how long your life is,
in compiling all that whiz.
If you're undergoing new stuff,
politely introduce it to the the old. Don't be rough
if the mingling starts to get tough.
Keep your brain clear
to allow new things in the new year.

WHO'S THERE REMAINING THAT MEMORY IS RETAINING?

Life is here today and gone tomorrow,
giving your surviving friends sorrow
that you'll no longer be around.
For some, your loss is considered profound,
since you're not there to be found.
Being contemporary is the basis of friendship,
otherwise it's a sunken ship.
If one friend is there, but the other's not,
it's an arrested friendship that can't untie the knot.
So let both parties remain alive
for the very friendship itself to survive.
What the remembering can really recall
is the dead one or two whom you loved above all,
or else it's three or four,
or else even more,
but it was never a loaded store
that your love can restore.
Or is it?
Let's resume our visit.
Maybe there's someone else, but you missed it.

**THE ESSENCE OF FRIENDSHIP
IS TO SAIL ON THE SAME SHIP
WITHOUT FALLING OFF THE DECK INTO THE DIP
BY WAY OF AN INADVERTENT SLIP**

Simply to be *with* your friend
is so satisfactory, you hope it doesn't end.
He's also comfortable in *your* presence,
as if you offer him presents.
So the two of you together
are a boost in any weather.
You're both attuned to the same wavelength,
which constitutes your relationship's extent,
being both directionally in the same bent.
Therefore to be separated with haste
is an annoying nuisance of waste.
So we prolong each other's company
to make each other feel extra comfy.

IS MEMORY FALSELY INAUTHENTIC, DEVIATING INTO THE WRONGLY ECCENTRIC?

(1)

If memory fails you,
why must it ail you?
Just because it doesn't prevail
is no reason why you should dump it in a pail,
if by now it only looks stale.

(2)

Memory keeps the past alive,
but only to a mental extent.
It can't revive the actual event
that you experienced in true life
to an even visceral degree.
Instead, by a sort of photograph,
it barely mimics an autograph.
So memory is really second-hand,
and reduces the vivid to the bland,
never being in total command
on this, our earthly land.
Life by itself is the real thing,
which memory can only approximately bring,
like a parked bird suddenly taking wing
surrounded by "atmosphere"
in the false earth's phony sphere.
Is memory really evidently here?
As time goes by, we're shut off,
so concrete reality turns abstractly soft,
no longer held in true substance aloft.

**OLD FRIENDS
GOT SAD ENDS**

What happened to my old friends?
They all came to sad ends,
which Death took charge of
in his proprietorial capacity
and aggressive personality.
Since my old friends were knocked off,
I can't boast that I'm better off.
I miss them enough to cry,
or weep, as the case may be.
They all loved me,
as I now love them in vain,
so the sum of their deaths is one immense pain
from which severe melancholy can't refrain.

**RELISHING ALL MY FRIENDS
DURING MY LONELY ENDS.
I WAS SO GREGARIOUS
THAT THEY WERE MULTIFARIOUS**

If my life is coming to an end,
I say goodbye to every friend,
all combined at once,
clad in the same poem.
I regret to leave you all
with a vertical fall
due to a balance flaw
that left me sprawled on the floor,
unconscious forever
after my life's full endeavor.
You friends ratified my life
and softened its eternal strife.
Now, having given up the ghost,
you friends glorified my life the most,
because with you it was fun and games,
although I've forgotten most of your names,
but you were a lovely bunch of guys and dames.
To leave you all is a bevy of shames
attached to my wholesale abandonment.
I must have cherished every grand minute
in your company that seemed so infinite.

DOES MEMORY HAVE TO FAIL, AND NOT QUITE AVAIL?

I can't see my dead old friends any more
except through memory, which will restore
their images alone,
not themselves flesh-and-bone.
I try to have conversation
with my old friends, but only in condensation,
by my making up their lines,
by imitating their remembered designs
of thinking and talking.
To repeat their exact words, I'm balking.
It's like shadowing a ghost,
but trying to make the most,
like having a regular toast
in praise of Friendship
that only memory will revive,
since only one of our pair could survive
to now be fully alive.
I'm the only one to actually be,
with organs functioning free.
Thus, through many tears,
I try to recapture those good old years,
but mainly fail, since they disappear
from all due relevance, in the rear.
At least I could drink that same old beer,
but it doesn't quite revive our essentially mutual cheer.
To myself I must make that clear.
But the image remains preciously dear.

MY OLD FRIENDS
HAVE ALL SEEN THEIR ENDS

I'm the only one who's left
to mourn them right and left.
When they were vividly alive,
my social life would thrive.
I'll join them in our massive memorial.
In our own journal I'll do the editorial,
saying what a generation we were,
to infinitely prefer.
As I write it, they all jump up and stir.
What do we all do? We reminisce and confer.
We remember old times
to celebrate our joys and crimes.
We all had such fun,
and weep when it's all done.
Each one was an individual
participating in the procedural,
delving in with a feature-al
to manifest his creature-al.

FRIENDSHIP

I loved old friends with all my heart.
Nostalgia gave them an extra special tint
or glow. Did they depart to go below?
Wherever or if ever did they go?
I search for them along Memory Lane.
An old friend is very difficult to explain.
They had a permanent grip on you,
beyond what you tripped along with them.
They touched your heart's sweet spots.
Your devotion to them was tops.
They all did you a favor.
Each one had a different flavor.
Your memory is their saver.
Some things take an ineffable toll
on your heart, when all is truly told.
Friendship is so emotional,
it could even verge on the devotional.
So don't take friendship lightly,
but it's quite all right to take it blithely
as it sails along so very slightly.
You could sing along to their singularity.
Friendship more than only stirred.
It actually poured out and purred.
Friendship had a special nature
of divine infrequency.
It was sacred with its secrecy.
There was the element of love
that placed it somehow above.
It had its own intimacy
sustained infinitely.
It wasn't just a one-time Charlie,

but lingered in its folly.
We often made plans,
but not all of them could land.
They couldn't be fulfilled
as it could have been billed.
We whisper love whistly
but it could have been crisply.
Where should we categorize it mystery
along the private roads of one's history?

LIKE A COW I GRAZE
ON THE GRASS OF OLD DAYS

Those dead days beyond repair
come up and gulp for air.
I'm with my old friends day and night
for their images to reignite.
I clutch and caress and bless
them all till my life is a mess
of ghosts that renew their shapes
like sweet and endless cherry grapes
for me to continually devour
till surfeit of them makes me sour
to recombat them hour by hour.
They combine their petals into one gigantic flower.

I FOUND HIM AND LOST HIM AGAIN

I dreamed of an old friend, dead for many years,
and suddenly he appears
as if that's the normal thing to do.
We acted with usual informality
as if imitating the dead reality,
and nothing had happened in between
those old days and the formation of this dream.
Everything was so real
as to be no big deal.
Our two lives were never broken.
It was Time, becoming an uncanny token
of friendship as usually spoken.
Thus I regained my old friend
only slightly, to delay unseemly end.
When the dream faded, the score
was the same as it was before.
He was only momentarily revived,
but never miraculously survived.

I WON'T GIVE IT AWAY.
GIVE WHAT AWAY?
SHAKESPEARE'S FAMOUS PLAY

The friendship between Hamlet and Horatio
was unequal, because Hamlet was nobility.
However, Horatio had a great ability
to be Hamlet's trusted friend,
until their friendship had to end,
because of a poisoned duel
after fighting with swords was so cruel.
Hamlet's death was the end of the play,
but not before he avenged his royal uncle
for poisoning the King, Hamlet's father.
However, I won't bother
to go any farther,
so I won't give away the play
in case you want to see it another day.
I'll keep Shakespeare's secret
by not letting you take a peep at it.
Since it's a good plot,
I haven't disturbed it a lot,
so you'll have to arrive at the beginning
to see if Prince Hamlet is winning.
Thus the tale of the play is spinning.

DISSECTING MEMORIES

Memories recapture the past
and renew its blast,
because of the way the mind is cast.
The past is where memories exist.
Some are vehement to persist
and remain on the lengthy list.
Some memories are not renewed
except for occasional views
that pop up here and there
when they come out for air,
so are kept on the back seat
with rarely a repeat.
Some memories are sad regrets,
the foul products of disastrous bets.
Some memories are reborn as dreams
before they come apart at the seams,
and lose their identity
when they're replaced by plenty
of alternate memories with their time to come
before eventually undone.
In conclusion, I declare
some memories are so vivid that you stare,
as though their reality was suddenly there.
You want to rub your eyes with awe,
so lifelike do they stand before,
as though invented on the spot,
so are frequently enjoyed a lot
when discharging their amazing plot.
Some memories, though, are absolute rot,
maybe because they're so ill-begot.
You bear your memories from the time you were a tot.

MEMORIES WERE MY CLOSE COMPANIONS.
THEY PLUNGED MY HILLS INTO CANYONS

Once I'm done,
my memories will be gone.
They've kept my company for so long.
What will I do without them?
They brought back what happened
with a reliable record.
They gave me constant consolation.
They put things in order, in place.
I frequently contemplated them.
My records have dropped out,
filing system and all.
Now I'm absent-minded,
not being reminded.
Since Death can obliterate memory,
need it do worse to inspire enmity?
Can Death have a worse fault
than to subject memory to assault
and then empty my whole vault?

ABRUPT NOCTURNAL HORROR

My friend Fred Gutzeit
is now out of sight.
He passed away in the middle of the night
hale and hearty—suddenly.
How could a body be so weak
as to turn so oblique?
His girlfriend Elizabeth tried to revive him,
but all she could do was survive him
across their shared beds,
and lost their spared threads.
What happened was aghast
and turned into the last
in this abrupt blast.
It happened too fast.
He was a beloved artist,
but that's only part of the list.
Elizabeth gave him her utmost assist
when together they were equally blissed.
By more than me, he's terribly missed.
I angrily defy fate with my raised fist.

WHAT A RELIEF!
WE WERE SPARED FROM GRIEF

I waited to meet my friend
at the appointed corner.
Between the avenue and the street
was where we were to meet.
But when he didn't show up,
had Death come to interrupt?
Whose life had Death taken?
In frenzy I was shaken.
If he's not at the appointed corner,
have I become his mourner?
He would have phoned if he was late.
Is this the closing of our gate?
But finally his form appeared,
and I was immediately cheered.
It turned out he was delayed.
So in restoration we played:
We engaged in conversation
after the near miss of devastation.
Thus the friendship resumed
as had been previously assumed.
Our expectation was met,
so no worry and no sweat.
Our talk was extra jolly,
being spared from tragic folly.

MY CURRENT SITUATION
IS NOT AN ENVIABLE STATION

I remember all my old friends
in three categories:
the known to be dead,
the still alive
(which includes me),
and the unknown if still alive.
I can't do visiting
or revisiting
because of a bum ticker
(my heart).
So I'm confined in staying home
(homebound).
So I'll ask some available friends to visit me.
So I have a limited social life
and an unlimited self life
along with my failing wife.
I'm stuck more than ever with old age,
and the end of the book barely has a readable page.
I've lived out life and am collecting my wage.
It's sparse and bare,
so I come out for air
while staying at home
with nowhere else to roam.
So here I am, stuck.
But social welfare gives me a buck
to elevate my lowly luck.

**A BENEVOLENT APPEAL
TO REDUCE SUFFERING'S ORDEAL**

Life is miserable for the sufferer,
but other people don't give a damn.
Friends can give you sympathy,
but strangers have no stake
in how you suffer for your own pitiful sake.
Compassion is not a common commodity
when pain is hardly an oddity.
Let the world take mercy's kindness
as an antidote to morality's blindness.

IF YOU THINK THAT YOU'RE THE BOSS, REMEMBER THAT YOU'VE ENDURED A LOSS

Life keeps obsessively driving ahead
from one thing to the next.
If the flow is stopped, you're vexed.
Its direction is always forward,
but retrospect is conducted backward
into the deep past
that's too far back to last.
So don't look too far behind,
so you'll lose your trend of mind,
or trip on something for being blind.
Then restore your projectory
and resume your search
in mathematical precision
that shouldn't be subtracted by division,
in which case you've lost your vision.
But you forgot what was your original mission.
Can I stumble back to retrieve it?
I'm at a loss. I can't believe it.

HOW TO CHOOSE YOUR FRIENDS, PRESUMING YOU'RE WORTHY OF THEM

If you're clever and bright,
seek the company of those who are likewise,
thus better able to appreciate your conversation.
If your friends are only stupid and dull,
they'll bring you down to the lowly level
of those dumb enough to discuss "God" and the devil.

SEEK YOUR OWN KIND,
WITH WHOM YOU'LL BE KINDER.
THIS IS A HAPPY REMINDER

I'm clever and bright.
So are you also seen in that light?

Yes, I have identical characteristics.
Therefore we'll understand each other's jokes,
both being compatible folks.

Not everyone gets along with everyone else.
We all seek harmonious relationships,
and reluctantly float any other ships.

Socializing is full of selection and preference.
Have you come with the right reference?

Of course. We're both in the same arena,
so with our similar demeanor,
we'll both land up serener.

We'll elevate our voices
to arrive at the same choices.

Since we compete in the same bout,
I'll never demean you by calling you a "lout,"
by way of a sneering adversarial shout,
resulting in our tragic falling out.

Good. Let's be friends forever.
Since we're both brilliant and clever,
we'll never be severed,
so neither will part,
and each be up to our compelling role

as part and parcel of each other's soul,
thus completing the dynamic whole.

That's friendship's definition
without a necessary partition.

LIFE AND DEATH ARE THE GREATEST DUO
WHEN THEY MATCH TOGETHER AS A FOE

Life is the greatest gift,
so I parcel out its abundance with thrift
from the number of years left
for my stealing not to be charged with theft.
I'm now of considerable old age,
venerable enough to be a sage.
The crowded stage is set
for me to remember old friends, you bet!
They're all dead, this whole bunch,
having vacated the premises for being out to lunch.
I'm intuitive enough to follow many a hunch.
I use the miracle of instinct
to make my eyes flutteringly blink,
giving me such views as to make me think
along the auspices of memory's mind
that brings back to consciousness my old grind.
In the past I'm happy to dwell
instead of being aghast by residing in Death's hell.
Better to be old with memory
than to be enlisted in Death when it succeeds in being my enemy
by defeating me and putting me underground
where my sorry old remains are too neglected to be found.
My poor old skull
is nothing but emptily dull.

HOW YOUR MENTAL MEMBER
HELPS YOU TO REMEMBER

You have to undergo an experience
in order to bring its memory into existence,
which is sometimes involuntary.
Now you know how memory works.
Your brain transforms what you underwent
into a recollection
of that particular session
to add to your permanent collection,
which you can resort to at any time
like a film pasted on your mind,
that replicates the remembered grind.
Being close at hand, it's easy to find.
You carry your brain at the top
as a handy vessel to contain what will pop,
and into your brain will it plop,
there to make a crucial stop,
and be there like a free public library,
but exclusively for you alone
to retain in your retentive skull bone
like a reminder on the telephone.

MEMORY'S ESSENCE
ERUPTS LIKE EFFERVESCENCE

Can memory go on forever,
with so much to choose from?

It's not like chewing gum,
or drinking gin or rum,
or just banging on a drum.
It bursts into the eardrum.

Memory has a wide range
and is very prone to change.

It's so evocative
as to be provocative.

I know I'm positively right
that memory sheds so much light
that I'm confused between day and night.

Am I up to it by being sufficiently bright?

I crank up memory some more.
How much variety can it store?

But if I'm sleepy, it can seem like a bore.
It makes me wonder: what's really at its core?

Is it photography?
Or a slice of geography?

It's full of transmogrify?

Is it its own trophy?
Can it ever revolt and go free?

**FRIENDSHIPS CAN BE PRAISED
WHEN ENERGETIC LEVELS ARE RAISED**

Friendships are great things to have.
You can't lose. They like you and you like them.
You and they exchange personalities
in entertaining conversations
full of condensations.
They give you their essences, you give them yours
with guaranteed wagging of the jaws,
even with laughter, like "hee-haws."
You leave each other so full of smiles
that the energy left over will sustain you for miles,
as to carry along nostalgically,
and what a false note would be apology!

MEMORIES DEPEND ON THE PAST
TO MAKE THEM VARIOUSLY LAST

It's great to have a past
that makes my memories last,
that are so worth saving.
They were so precious, I'm still raving
to record them diligently, by and by.
Some are so poignant, they make me cry.
Some are so shameful, I defy,
which if somebody recalls them, I deny,
Thus the past is a mixed bag.
It could make me brag, but also sag.
If I were a dog, they'd make my tail wag,
but in which direction?
I'll carve them apart, by section,
and play favorites, by election
from my bountiful collection.
Most valuable was my selection.
Memories are a sheer delight
to make me see clear through old light.

DESERVING PRAISE
I HAPPILY RAISE

Is Steve Klein an exceptionally nice guy?
Just don't ask why.
He's kind and good in every way
while helping others thrive.
Is there a better one alive?
Hard to tell. There are so many candidates
to win the first class prize.
That he's one of them is no surprise.
As far as virtues go, he's fully supplied.
The world is much poorer if he ever died.
With such high estimates, I've never lied.

IS IT STILL CHEWABLE ENOUGH TO BE RENEWABLE?

To see old friends after many years
disperses my petty fears
that I'm unworthy of holding on to,
as maintaining in the rank of friends,
so knowing them has come to its ends?
No. They still claim me as worthwhile
because they still fancy my style.
Thus, happy days are here again,
the past renewed as acceptably unbroken.
I hope it's not a mere guilty token
on their forgiving part
to revive me to the ranks of friendship's old art,
which is ever renewable
if only excusable.
But the past remains.
What did I ever do wrong
that now we seem to get along?
Can it be commemorated by song?
This is a question of old and new time
to see if they fit together in the same rhyme,
and not be categorized as a crime.

THE FUNERAL LESSON

If you get too old, the penalty is to die.
At your funeral, your old friends had a good cry,
then went home, feeling smug
to miss forever your friendly old mug,
which they had to write off now with a shrug.
From your example they learned not to get old
by sticking their necks out and getting too bold,
therefore joining the enormity of Death's hold,
which was a sobering lesson
at that funeral session.
They learned not to emulate
the replication of your grim fate,
which came sooner rather than late,
due to being at an earlier date.
Why does Death have to pull its weight
to put you in an unfortunate state
at an all-consuming rate?

MUTUALITY IS RETALIATORY.
IT'S A TWO-WAY GLORY
AS A SUBSTANTIAL STORY

Here's a reminder
for everyone to be kinder.
Then they're entitled to be beneficiaries
of your contributories.
It's a system of give and take
for everyone to be on the make.
Everyone owes you
if you already gave,
because they're in debt
to repay.
Not everything goes your way.
First you've got to be kind
for others to bear that in mind.
It's a two-way process.
Are we all making progress?
Yes, let's all co-operate
as the fairest way to operate.

WE'RE CARING BUDDIES

Your body is both the outside and inside of you, and nobody cares about it so intimately as you yourself.

So safeguard it against accidents? You bet!

And don't allow malicious germs inside to contaminate the well being of its elaborate organic construction.

Don't allow time to weaken to old age too swiftly, or else you'll have nothing left, leaving your personal death to have a picnic at your expense on unhealthy leftovers.

I get your message. It's straight and clear. Is your advice mainly for yourself or for me?

We're in the same boat.

I appreciate your going out of your way, using me as your proxy, or vice versa.

You're the very image of my alternate.

Mutual benevolence and gratitude feature our wholesome friendship, which to evacuate leaves me a total ingrate.

Thanks for watching out over me, which is self-care to encapsulate both.

TOO MUCH NOSTALGIA

Too much nostalgia
can give me neuralgia.
It's all too fond of the past
that was such a blast,
but I can't repeat it.
Instead it gets deleted
by my being without it.
I wish I wouldn't doubt it,
but to me it's turned its back.
I wish it would come back
and not tease me with its lack.
I long for what was,
so why does it withhold its old buzz?
For nostalgia I long,
but it's turned off its old song,
and I think that's damned wrong.
The past is giving me a fit
because presently it doesn't fit.
From me it's begun to split.
Can't I have a little bit,
which is so desirable from where I sit?
Please, oh please: don't omit.

NOSTALGIA YEARNS

Nostalgia yearns for the inaccessible,
which once was so easily gettable.
You're blocked off by circumstances
that don't permit you any such answers
that used to get you what you wanted,
but now difficulties are confronted.
Oh, those were the good old days
when the sun was full of vital rays,
and you didn't meet with such dismays.
Why are those solutions so lost
that your very will is being bossed?
Every hopeless struggle is at a high cost.
Come down with a case of neuroagia
to frustrate those bitter bouts of nostalgia.

LIFE AND DEATH COMPARED.
THEIR DIFFERENCES AREN'T SPARED

Anybody who succumbs to death
loses more than his mere breath.
He loses the mental might of memories,
whether permanent or temporaries.
The memories are like a movie,
whether old-fashioned or groovy.
The audience are glued to their seats,
counting their irregular heartbeats.
The memories get weirder and weirder,
like psychoanalysis becoming theater.
Life is quite a drama,
to justify all its clamor
as a unique personal glamour.
Death is a regular killjoy
in its obsession to destroy.
It does such a good job
that it infects the whole mob
worried about vascular throb.
Death is such a frightening prospect
that every future victim will vehemently object.
Life is infinitely preferred.
Whoever invented Death erred.

SAYING GOODBYE

Life is wonderful, but I got too old
to hold on to it for much longer.
I fear my deathday
when it will come what may.
I'll hurry up with my terminal memories
to feast on them quick before too late.
I'll wrap things up on my slate.
I'm jittery and nervous
to leave my New York flat,
therefore not impervious.
To friends lucky to survive me,
I say: "I wish you could revive me."
But they lack that capacity,
so I'll never die happily.
Being in Death's captivity
will curtail all my activity.
Therefore, goodbye, old world.
Glad to have given you a whirl.
It was very worthwhile,
so I now leave with half a smile.

**THE DUBIOUS END
COMES ROUND THE BEND**

The survivors grow ever fewer from our generation,
till memories are my only consolation.
But they're faint and weak compared with the actual person.
Dead friends offer no nourishment
in bolstering up one's punishment,
for what crime? For being born too early,
as I suffer solitude so surly.
I get no glory joining friends in Death,
while I'd rather feed conversation with my living breath.
Thus my ends in life are the saddest,
while early portions celebrate gladness.
Life is uneasily distributed,
since youth mainly had contributed.
So Death is not so anticlimactic
in the woes and travails of making life click,
once we've learned that useless trick
to build our mansion brick by brick,
so belatedly it's too late
to improve our halting fate
with some inspiration to create
some surprisingly acceptable state,
including of course a loving mate.

THE PAST
SEEMS ALWAYS TO LAST

"We were so happy!"
Those are the words that kill.
They have the skill
to renew the presence of past events
as if still true today.
Too much power they yield
to bring back old fields
of flowers, and scenes on which we walked,
and in all seasons talked
when in our presence we created cheer
within the vicinity of being near.
All that was too long ago.
Oh, I miss you so!
Your absence is my eternal foe
when mentally we continue to go.

OLD AGE IS WORSE THAN YOUTH.
THIS IS REGARDED AS THE TRUTH

Nostalgia and grief
need not be brief.
I spend many sessions
undergoing depressions.
My best years of life are already past.
I knew they wouldn't last.
I have to swallow the bitter pill of old age
without having to have a tirade and a rage.
My best years are gone.
Needless to dwell upon.
But dwell I indeed do.
They give sweet and sour nostalgia.
Is that a disease, like neuralgia?
I don't know medical terms.
All I do is collect germs.
Will they ruin my whole system?
Then how can I get out of it? Any wisdom?

GRIEF AND NOSTALGIA

Grief and nostalgia refer to wonderful times in the past
involving your great pals, but those days didn't last.
And now you're desperate for their being renewed,
but they're inaccessible and can't be viewed.
They haunt you because they're no longer there for you.
And their yearning for you is just as acute.
Those invariably good old days never returned.
But if they or you could only have them back!
The distress is due to that unappeasable lack.
Here today and gone tomorrow
is the sheer definition of sorrow.
Those great pals were your soul-mates,
and you uniquely were theirs.
For them you retain an eternally recurring taste,
which makes for you their excruciating waste.
If only they could rejoin you by magic,
but you and they remain perversely tragic!
To want ferociously and not get
is of all dooms the costliest debt.
Therefore woe are nostalgia and grief
which persist miserably without relief.

BROAD STAGES OF LIFE, GENERALIZED AND SIMPLIFIED

(Characters: two old men.)

Growing up in youth is a matter of learning about new adventures.

Living through old age is a matter about remembering the past, including nostalgia, and prolonged grief for missing old friends.

Yeah. First comes the learning youth. Then comes the remembering old age. In between those periods is a mixture of both.

Well, that just about sums up the broad stages of life.

In old age there's another factor besides memory. It's fear of death.

Which gets more as time grows closer to that culmination.

Time has a lot to encompass. It's called "lifetime."

Before the end comes adjusting and rolling with the punches, getting physically weaker all the time.

Any conclusion about life?

Yeah. Thanks, parents. It was a great lucky break. Sorry for "using" you. I hope it wasn't too bad from your end, either.

Afterword

WRITTEN ON THE DAY MARVIN AND I DECIDED TO GET MARRIED

Walking through the Brooklyn Botanic Gardens in mid-March:
Over there are crocuses, and here are snowdrops, dangling
     prettily;
But the trees are still bare—
Until you get up close.

Some buds are eighth-of-an-inch duck heads, sleek, flat;
Some are miniature asparagus tops;
Others fuzzy dark-blue caterpillars
Or velvety pussywillow buttons;
Still others wrapped flame-nuggets.

We ran out of words
When we thought of these little tips
Holding
A sky full of blossoms.

Candace Watt 3/17/86: Marvin and I were married 5/22/86

Marvin Cohen is the author of four novels, a book on baseball, a collection of plays, and several volumes of short pieces, dialogues and verse.

His shorter work has appeared in over 100 magazines and books, including: *Ambit, Antaeus, Assembling, Center Magazine, Cricket Addict's Archive, Essaying Essays, Exacting Clam, Extensions, Harper's Bazaar, Hudson Review, Monks Pond, The Nation, National Camp Director's Guide, New Directions in Prose and Poetry, New York Times, Plays from the New York Shakespeare Festival, Pushcart Prize, Quarterly Review of Literature, Salmagundi, Sun and Moon, Transatlantic Review, Village Voice, Vogue (UK)*, and *Wormwood Review*.

His writing ranges from the experimental to fable; from poetry to prose; from internal dialogues to playscripts; from art criticism to cricket fandom; from humour to philosophical essays, and from aesthetics to surrealism (he says "if people say so then it must be true").

Born in Brooklyn in 1931, Cohen has described himself as one who has "risen from lower-class background to lower-class foreground." He studied art at Cooper Union but left college to focus on writing, supporting himself with a series of odd jobs, from mink farmer to merchant seaman. He later taught creative writing at various New York colleges, including The New School, the City College of New York and Adelphi University.

For a long time, Marvin Cohen has lived in East Village of Manhattan.

www.ingramcontent.com/pod-product-compliance
Lightning Source LLC
Chambersburg PA
CBHW020330170426
43200CB00006B/334